Advance Praise for Eating Disorders

"Collectively, Walsh, Attia and Glasofer have been at the cutting edge of eating disorders treatment and research for several decades now. These authors are extraordinarily well placed to provide a wide ranging and informative text on everything someone with an eating disorder, or someone who cares for a loved one with an eating disorder ought to know. Ultimately, this text serves as the perfect psychoeducational volume to empower sufferers and their carers to take the necessary step(s) in the recovery process."

—**Daniel Le Grange**, PhD, Benioff UCSF Professor in Children's Health, Department of Psychiatry, UCSF, CA, and Emeritus Professor of Psychiatry and Behavioral Neuroscience, The University of Chicago, Chicago, IL

"Written by an internationally acclaimed team of clinical researchers, this book is a comprehensive update on the science of eating disorder and its relevance for clinical care for people with an eating disorder. This book is a must read resource for anyone who wants to gain an accurate understanding of eating disorders: what they are, what can be done to prevent them, and how best to support people who experience an eating disorders or have a loved one who is affected."

— **Ruth Striegel Weissman**, Dipl Psych, PhD, Editor-in-Chief, *International Journal of Eating Disorders*

"Written by a team of top clinician-researchers, this outstanding practical guide covers what eating disorders are and are not and what we know and don't know about them – It delivers a clear and concise road map to the most effective evidence-based treatments and to finding help for you or your loved one."

—**Angela S. Guarda**, MD, Stephen and Jean Robinson Associate Professor of Eating Disorders, Department of Psychiatry, Johns Hopkins University School of Medicine

EATING DISORDERS

WHAT EVERYONE NEEDS TO KNOW®

B. TIMOTHY WALSH
EVELYN ATTIA
DEBORAH R. GLASOFER

OXFORD
UNIVERSITY PRESS

OXFORD
UNIVERSITY PRESS

Oxford University Press is a department of the University of Oxford. It furthers the University's objective of excellence in research, scholarship, and education by publishing worldwide. Oxford is a registered trade mark of Oxford University Press in the UK and certain other countries.

"What Everyone Needs to Know" is a registered trademark of Oxford University Press.

Published in the United States of America by Oxford University Press 198 Madison Avenue, New York, NY 10016, United States of America.

Library of Congress Cataloging-in-Publication Data
Names: Walsh, B. Timothy, 1946– author. | Attia, Evelyn, author. |
Glasofer, Deborah R., 1979– author.
Title: Eating disorders : what everyone needs to know / B. Timothy Walsh,
Evelyn Attia, Deborah R. Glasofer.
Description: New York : Oxford University Press, [2020] |
Series: What everyone needs to know |
Includes bibliographical references and index.
Identifiers: LCCN 2019048252 (print) | LCCN 2019048253 (ebook) |
ISBN 9780190926601 (paperback) | ISBN 9780190926595 (hardback) |
ISBN 9780190926625 (epub)
Subjects: LCSH: Eating disorders. | Eating disorders—Treatment. |
Eating disorders—Prevention.
Classification: LCC RC552.E18 W35 2020 (print) | LCC RC552.E18 (ebook) |
DDC 616.85/26—dc23
LC record available at https://lccn.loc.gov/2019048252
LC ebook record available at https://lccn.loc.gov/2019048253

1 3 5 7 9 8 6 4 2
Paperback printed by LSC Communications, United States of America
Hardback printed by Bridgeport National Bindery, Inc., United States of America

CONTENTS

ACKNOWLEDGMENTS

We are grateful to the patients and families we have worked with over the years who have taught us so much, inspired us to keep asking questions, and reminded us that full recovery from eating disorders is possible. Thanks as well to Sarah Harrington at Oxford University Press for suggesting we undertake this project, reading chapters along the way, and giving us excellent feedback. And finally thanks to the community of colleagues, at Columbia and other institutions nationally and internationally, without whom knowledge about eating disorders would not advance.

PART I

FACING THE FACTS AND
BUSTING THE MYTHS

1

WHAT ARE EATING DISORDERS?

The term *eating disorders* refers to a group of illnesses characterized by disturbances in eating and eating-related behaviors. Eating disorders pose significant risks to physical health and negatively impact day-to-day functioning (for example, at school or work or in relationships) and are widely considered to be the most dangerous of mental disorders.

How are eating disorders diagnosed?

The *Diagnostic and Statistical Manual of Mental Disorders* (DSM) is a publication of the American Psychiatric Association (APA) and is written with input from a large number of clinical experts—not just psychiatrists—in different specialty areas related to mental health. The DSM describes the signs and symptoms of all psychiatric conditions and provides criteria to guide treatment providers in deciding whether an individual has a recognized mental disorder. The DSM has been in use since 1952, and the current, fifth edition, DSM-5, was published in 2013. Each revision to the DSM has been aimed at improving the usefulness of the manual.

Eating disorders are considered psychiatric illnesses and are therefore listed in the DSM-5. Eating disorders are listed in a section called "Feeding and Eating Disorders." But, as a shorthand, we are going to refer to all the disorders in this section of the DSM-5 as eating disorders. The diagnostic criteria for eating disorders in the DSM-5 are different from what came before, in DSM-IV; in the DSM-5, changes were made that aimed to clarify some items and to make the criteria relevant to all groups of patients (for example, adolescents as well as adults, males as well as females).

The DSM-5 is used by mental health professionals (also referred to here as *clinicians*) to help make a formal diagnosis, and it allows all health providers to use the same criteria when they assess someone who may have an eating disorder. However, clinicians are urged to use it as a guidebook, not a bible. As a result, clinicians always use their experience and best judgment to decide whether a particular patient has or does not have a particular diagnosis.

What is on the list of eating disorders?

The eating disorders described in the DSM-5 are anorexia nervosa, bulimia nervosa, binge-eating disorder, avoidant/restrictive food intake disorder (ARFID), pica, and rumination disorder.

The hallmark feature of *anorexia nervosa* (often referred to simply as *anorexia*) is a reduced consumption of calories that results in

- an abnormally low weight for adults or a failure for children and teens to grow as they should,
- a fear of weight gain or of becoming fat (or an inability to eat in a way that supports a healthy weight), and
- a distortion of or overemphasis on body weight and shape.

People with this disorder commonly have difficulty recognizing the seriousness of not eating enough for their body's needs.

Approximately 50% of adults with anorexia nervosa also binge eat and/or purge regularly. *Purging* refers to inappropriate behaviors that aim to compensate for food consumed and can involve self-induced vomiting or misuse of medicines like laxatives, diuretics, or enemas.

Bulimia nervosa (also called *bulimia*) is a disorder in which people whose weights are within or above the normal range engage in repeated episodes of binge eating and purging. These episodes occur on average at least once weekly over a 3-month time frame. It is important to emphasize that although the term *binge* is sometimes used colloquially to mean overdoing it with food, when it comes to discussing eating disorders, *binge-eating* has a very specific meaning. A binge-eating episode involves feeling out of control (i.e., feeling as though it's nearly impossible to stop) while eating an amount of food that most people would agree is large given the circumstances.

Individuals with bulimia nervosa attempt to compensate for binge eating by

- vomiting,
- fasting,
- exercising, and/or
- misusing medicines like laxatives.

These compensatory behaviors may also occur outside of binge-eating episodes. Similar to those with anorexia nervosa, people with bulimia nervosa are very concerned with and focused on their body weight and shape. These aspects of appearance are a major factor in how people with this disorder think and feel about themselves, and severe unhappiness with how they think they look is common.

People with *binge-eating disorder* regularly engage in binge-eating episodes like those just described, but they do not purge.

During binge-eating episodes, people with binge-eating disorder commonly eat

- faster than usual,
- until they are very full,
- when they are not hungry, and
- alone, because they are ashamed or embarrassed about how much they eat.

The experience of binge eating can be very upsetting. Most, but not all, adults with this disorder who come for treatment are overweight or obese. While some people with binge-eating disorder may feel very concerned about their body weight or shape, this is neither universal nor required to meet criteria for the disorder.

People with *ARFID* eat in a highly restrictive manner, sometimes resulting in low weight or medical problems. But, unlike individuals with anorexia nervosa, those with ARFID avoid certain foods based on sensory features, such as texture or color, because of fears related to the process of eating, such as choking, or because of lack of interest in food and eating—not because of concern about getting fat, body shape, or weight.

Pica refers to the phenomenon of repeatedly eating nonnutritive food substances, such as dirt, paint, or paper, in a developmentally and contextually inappropriate way. For example, a toddler or an individual living in famine would not be considered to have pica if non-food substances were repeatedly eaten.

Rumination disorder is characterized by the repeated regurgitation of food (that is, bringing food that has just been swallowed back up into the mouth), which is not explained by another eating disorder or by a medical condition.

The DSM-5 also briefly describes a set of *other specified feeding and eating disorders* (OSFED). These disorders are significant because they get in the way of day-to-day functioning and are very distressing to the individual. They are considered "other" simply because relatively little is known about them and more research is needed to understand their characteristics and complications and how best to define them.

Examples of OSFED described in DSM-5 are as follows:

- Atypical anorexia nervosa
- Subthreshold bulimia nervosa
- Subthreshold binge-eating disorder
- Purging disorder
- Night eating syndrome

People with atypical anorexia nervosa exhibit all the behavioral and psychological symptoms of classic anorexia nervosa, including notable weight loss, but are not technically underweight according to guidelines provided by the Centers for Disease Control and Prevention (CDC). Individuals with this OSFED often may have been overweight or obese prior to the start of their condition and have lost substantial weight as part of their disorder, and perhaps can be thought of as underweight based on their own body's needs. They therefore strongly resemble individuals with typical anorexia nervosa and are at risk for developing some of the physical complications associated with anorexia nervosa. Individuals with subthreshold bulimia nervosa and binge-eating disorder engage in binge eating and purging as described earlier, but at a frequency of less than once weekly. The primary features of purging disorder are inappropriate compensatory behaviors such as self-induced vomiting after eating small or normal amounts of food, and excessive concern about body shape and weight. For people with night eating syndrome, the primary problem is repeatedly eating the majority of their food throughout the evening, sometimes including episodes of waking up in the middle of the night to eat.

Table 1.1. ICD-10 codes for the feeding and eating disorders

Disorder	ICD-10
Anorexia nervosa	F. 50.0
Unspecified	F. 50.00
Restricting type	F. 50.01
Binge-eating/purging type	F. 50.02
Bulimia nervosa	F. 50.2
Binge-eating disorder	F. 50.81
Other specified feeding and eating disorder	F. 50.89
Avoidant/restrictive food intake disorder	F. 50.82
Pica	F. 98.3 (children)
	F. 50.8 (adults)
Rumination disorder	F. 98.21
Eating disorder, unspecified	F. 50.9

Since the United States is a member of the World Health Organization (WHO), when clinicians in the United States describe the illness for which a patient is receiving treatment they are required to use a code listed in a publication known as the *International Classification of Diseases* (ICD), 10th edition. These codes are used for billing purposes for medical and mental healthcare visits, and the code numbers are likely to be on a bill generated by a provider for an evaluation or treatment session. Although the DSM-5 is published in the United States by the APA, the DSM-5 provides guidance for which ICD codes correspond to each eating disorder (see Table 1.1).

Why are so many eating disorders described in DSM-5?

It may seem confusing and surprising that there are so many labels for disorders that have so much in common. For example, both anorexia nervosa and bulimia nervosa primarily affect young women, and people with both disorders have a lot of concerns about body shape and weight and try hard to restrict calories. The reason the DSM-5 distinguishes them is that, despite their impressive similarities, there are major differences: people with anorexia nervosa are much more likely to develop physical complications than those with bulimia nervosa, and people with bulimia nervosa tend to respond better to treatment with either medication or therapy than those with anorexia nervosa.

Generally, the eating disorders defined in the DSM-5 differ significantly from one another in their complications, how the illness changes with time, and how it responds to treatment.

What eating problems are not on the list?

There are a number of eating behaviors and attitudes commonly described in popular culture that are not, in and of themselves, considered disorders. Chief among these is dieting. In the United States, an estimated 50 million people start a diet each January. Contemporary thinking about health has led to many ideas about how to reduce how much or what people eat: juice cleanses, vegetarianism and veganism, gluten-free diets (in the absence of celiac disease), and protein-rich/low-carbohydrate Atkins or Paleo plans. A number of these approaches are based on weak evidence, and they can be limiting and time consuming for dieters and irritating to others in their midst, but they are not considered to be illnesses. The majority of dieters abandon their diets after a few weeks. Others apply dietary practices flexibly and in ways that do not otherwise disrupt their physical or psychological well-being. However, in some vulnerable individuals, dietary guidelines become increasingly rigid and impairing, resulting in a transition from diet to disorder.

Orthorexia, a term introduced at the end of the twentieth century, refers to an unhealthy obsession with healthy eating, like being very concerned with a food's quality, origins, or preparation. Orthorexia per se is not recognized as an eating disorder. But if the food obsessions described as orthorexia make it hard to maintain a healthy weight or lead to the development of medical problems, a diagnosis of anorexia nervosa or of ARFID may apply. If the highly restrictive eating behavior growing out of orthorexic attitudes results in reactive binge-eating episodes, a diagnosis of bulimia nervosa, binge-eating disorder, or OSFED may apply.

Diabulimia describes the phenomenon of insulin misuse by people with type 1 diabetes for the purpose of weight control. This can take the form of skipping doses of insulin to lose weight or increasing doses of insulin to compensate for binge-eating episodes. This behavior can be incredibly dangerous medically and may signal that someone is overly upset about body shape or weight. Diabulimia is not its own diagnostic category because there are already two eating disorder diagnoses that can be used to capture the most extreme constellation of symptoms. In the case that an individual's insulin misuse results in an underweight state and in fear or inability to improve weight, a diagnosis of anorexia nervosa likely applies. If someone is maintaining their weight but relying on insulin "overdosing" as a compensatory behavior following binge-eating episodes, a diagnosis of bulimia nervosa is likely warranted.

Obesity is not considered an eating disorder. The term *obesity* refers to the presence of excess body fat, which usually results from higher energy intake (i.e., caloric consumption) relative to expenditure (i.e., physical activity) over many years. Obesity is not considered a mental disorder because a range of factors—biological, behavioral, and environmental—that vary across people contribute to its development. Poverty might be considered a crude analogy. A few people live in poverty because of some behavioral problem that prevents them from holding down a job. But poverty is, for the most part, the result of external forces and factors such as the state of the economy and the job market.

Why do we need so many different labels?

It may seem strange that there are so many different categories of eating disorders, especially since there is overlap in symptoms across the different disorders. The labels are clinically useful, however, when describing patients who are similar in what they can expect to happen to them and in which treatments will work for them. For example, people with anorexia nervosa have similarities in the age at which their illness develops (adolescence and young adulthood), the medical problems that may develop as part of the condition, and the treatments that work, all of which are different from the experience of individuals with another eating disorder.

Are we sure these labels are right?

Ever since the first publication of the DSM, there has been a process of reviewing and editing the list of diagnostic labels, using the latest information about the identified illness such as course, causes, and responsivity to treatment. A current debate about the role of weight range in the diagnosis of anorexia nervosa has the field and affected individuals wondering how future versions of the DSM may settle this score. While the diagnostic criteria for anorexia nervosa has always included mention of significantly low body weight, the clarification to the diagnostic language used in the most recently published diagnostic manual (DSM-5) emphasizes that there is no specific weight cutoff that defines anorexia nervosa. Clinicians must consider an individual's weight history, growth trajectory, ethnic background, and other aspects when determining whether his or her weight is significantly low.

This change has led to debate among providers and patients alike about whether anorexia nervosa can exist in a large-bodied person. In other words, should a person whose body mass index (BMI, calculated as weight in kilograms/[height in meters]^2) is higher than average for age, ethnic background, and other criteria be considered for the diagnosis of anorexia nervosa if the person has previously lost weight and developed the thoughts and behaviors that are typical of anorexia nervosa, such as a fear of fat and a preoccupation with body shape and weight? According to DSM-5, the formal diagnosis of anorexia nervosa is reserved for individuals whose weight is lower than average and likely lower than what most clinicians would consider minimally expected. The label of *atypical anorexia nervosa* is used for individuals who meet all but the weight criteria, and therefore would be the likely clinical term used for a larger-bodied individual with the symptoms just described.

Defining normal weight has become more complicated as the average weight for the population has increased in recent years. In fact, there has been interest in the idea of "health at every size" (HAES). This label is based on a book of that name, written in 2008 by Linda Bacon, which proposes that normal weight is different for different individuals and describes how dieting behaviors can often lead to unhealthy results. The emphasis in HAES is on achieving improved health and quality of life using a plan to enhance healthy eating behaviors together with body acceptance. Some supporters of the HAES approach prefer that language about weight recommendations, or the idea of "normal" weight, be removed from educational materials about eating disorders. In fact, the field itself has found the terminology confusing since "normal" weight may mean what is characteristic for the largest proportion of the population (i.e., increasing numbers in recent years) as well as what connotes healthy and/or desirable. It is important to acknowledge that holistic health may not be the same as medical health and that a high weight may be optimally healthy for some individuals.

As for diagnosis, providers (and insurance companies) rely on DSM-5 and ICD-10 terminology. We therefore have included discussion of weight criteria for anorexia nervosa and mention of definitions of "normal" weight in relevant sections of this book. As mentioned, individuals who meet all but the low weight criteria for anorexia nervosa, receive the diagnosis of atypical anorexia nervosa.

What are the common, core elements across eating disorders?

Aberrant eating behavior and behavior related to eating are the core, common features across distinct eating disorders. Of course, the type of unusual eating behavior can vary widely (see Table 1.2).

The secondary core element of all eating disorders is the mental distress underlying, accompanying, or resulting from disturbances in eating behavior. Perfectionism, low self-esteem, and a lot of worry about appearance—body shape, weight, or both—often (but not always) set off a change in eating behavior. Once the behavior becomes routine, the psychological distress intensifies and people typically become *more* rigid, *less* confident in themselves, and *more* focused on and dissatisfied with appearance. Guilt or shame about eating is commonplace and persistent. Finally, a distorted sense of control tends to accompany eating disorders. Across the different diagnoses, from ARFID to binge-eating disorder, feelings like panic or loss of control are experienced when eating foods that are not considered safe. In anorexia nervosa and

Table 1.2. Common elements across eating disorders

	Examples
Eating Pattern	• Skipping meals • Strict rules about what or when to eat • Food choices influenced by goals of restriction, weight loss, or binge-purge behaviors • Limited variety in diet • Eating in isolation or avoiding social occasions • Inattentiveness to hunger and/or fullness cues • Inducing vomiting after eating
Eating Behavior	• Pace of eating (i.e., very slowly or quickly) • Unusual combinations of foods selected • Determining what or how much to eat in relation to perceptions of what others think, or what they are doing

bulimia nervosa, there is a belief that paying a lot of attention to food or restriction of food equals control, even as the behaviors of illness take hold (i.e., control) of the individual and get in the way of day-to-day functioning.

What does normal eating look like?

Normal eating is regular, balanced, and flexible. By *regular*, we mean that the pattern of eating involves multiple meals and snacks daily, essentially eating every three to four hours, and remaining attuned to feelings of hunger and fullness. *Balanced* refers to the composition of one's diet—inclusive of protein, fat, and carbohydrate—and, by extension, a variety of foods. Normal eating is typically also a result of balanced attention to food content and preference; foods may be chosen because of their nutritional value, because they smell and taste yummy, or some combination of the two. Eating *flexibly* involves adapting to the needs of the situation. Examples of flexibility with eating include eating at a different time than planned and being able to eat adequately from options of non-preferred foods in social situations or when traveling. Holidays tend also to be occasions when normal eating is characterized by eating flexibly in terms of what, when, and how much; many of us eat differently (often more, and less balanced!) during the holidays.

There are behavioral, psychological, and social elements to normal eating, just as with disordered eating. Mentally, normal eating is characterized by an ability to take pleasure in food and to *just eat* at times, by the absence of guilt in anticipation of food, and by not being hyper-aware or hyper-unaware of each bite during a meal. When eating normally, people tend not to overthink about what or how much was eaten, and they avoid highly critical feelings about themselves related to their eating. People without eating disorders may sometimes eat in response to positive or negative emotions, for example, celebrating a work raise or feeling upset after an argument with a spouse, but this occurs neither frequently nor with great intensity.

What is the difference between an eating disorder and disordered eating?

Eating behavior and attitudes about appearance can be thought of as being on a spectrum from normal, to disordered eating, to eating disorders (see Figure 1.1). In the case of disordered eating, decisions about what to eat are sometimes influenced by a desire to maintain a certain weight or body type, and this can occasionally lead to guilt when things "don't go as planned," either in terms of foods eaten or weight or body shape changes. Hunger and fullness cues are commonly ignored, and eating occurs in response to emotion with some regularity. Vigilance about eating is common. For example, an individual may frequently compare what or how much she or he is eating in relation to a companion, and wind up under-eating or feeling bad about eating behavior. Or, a person

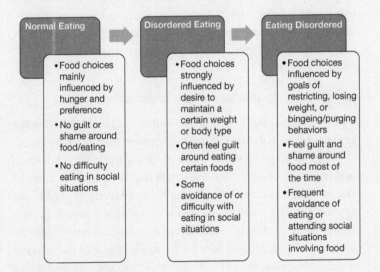

Normal Eating
- Food choices mainly influenced by hunger and preference
- No guilt or shame around food/eating
- No difficulty eating in social situations

Disordered Eating
- Food choices strongly influenced by desire to maintain a certain weight or body type
- Often feel guilt around eating certain foods
- Some avoidance of or difficulty with eating in social situations

Eating Disordered
- Food choices influenced by goals of restricting, losing weight, or bingeing/purging behaviors
- Feel guilt and shame around food most of the time
- Frequent avoidance of eating or attending social situations involving food

Figure 1.1. Eating behavior spectrum.

may spend a lot of time counting calories and researching the calories and macronutrients in foods prior to or after eating. Another type of hyper-awareness is directly linking food intake and exercise, for example, feeling compelled to run for an hour because of what or how much was eaten at the last meal. Disordered eating attitudes also often involve a good food–bad food mindset.

With eating disorders, food choice is primarily influenced by a desire to cut back and lose weight and/or by binge-purge behaviors. Emotions play a large part in eating behavior, whether this takes the form of eating too much to numb out or self-soothe, or eating too little to avoid anxiety, guilt, or shame. Eating often occurs in isolation or in secret, and social occasions involving food are avoided. The problematic attitudes about food are linked to behaviors such as measuring and weighing food, severely limiting food variety, or making strict rules about the timing of meals. Many people with eating disorders will, at least for a time, play down or deny the problems they are experiencing because of these behaviors, even when they are putting their physical health at risk. In the case of a formal eating disorder, the focus on food and weight directly impacts many important areas of a person's life, including relationships with others.

Why does it matter whether someone has an eating disorder?

We, of course, believe that it matters very much whether someone has an eating disorder. There are many reasons why.

First, eating disorders take a toll physically. Anorexia nervosa, for example, has one of the highest mortality rates of any psychiatric illness. According to an analysis of 36 studies, a young woman with this disorder faces six times the average risk of death for someone her age, and mortality rises by 5% for every decade of illness. Remaining at too low a body weight has profound consequences on the function and structure of the cardiovascular system. Abnormal heart rhythms, called *arrhythmias,* can develop, as well as low blood pressure and decreased heart size. Individuals with the variant of OSFED called atypical anorexia nervosa may also develop problems with heart and blood pressure similar to those seen in classic anorexia nervosa, because people with this OSFED are at a lower weight than what their body needs to function normally. The underweight state can also result in poor bone health, even in young people, and in women, disrupts menstrual functioning and fertility.

A symptom common to anorexia nervosa binge-purge subtype, bulimia nervosa, and some OSFEDs such as purging disorder and subthreshold bulimia nervosa is the presence of some type of inappropriate compensatory behavior. Be it vomiting or misuse of medicines like laxatives and diuretics (water pills), these behaviors contribute to dehydration and loss of crucial electrolytes (salts such as potassium and sodium) from the body. In addition, frequent vomiting can lead to dental erosion and tears in the esophagus.

The frequent binge-eating episodes characteristic of bulimia nervosa and binge-eating disorder may contribute, in some individuals, to excessive weight gain over time. This may contribute to the risk of medical problems.

Eating disorders also take a toll psychologically. Individuals with eating disorders often feel depressed and anxious, and not solely about eating and body weight and shape. A sense of hopelessness about the possibility of lasting recovery is common, as is fear and anxiety about the process of behavior change. People with anorexia nervosa are eight times more likely to attempt suicide than those in the general population. In addition, approximately one-third of adults with bulimia nervosa have had thoughts of suicide, with 25–30% having made attempts.

The medical risk and sense of despair associated with eating disorders make it very important to identify these problems. After identification, engagement in treatment is the next critical step. Current research suggests that only about 50% of people who meet criteria for an eating disorder have sought treatment. And yet, as we will discuss later on, effective treatments are available, and full recovery is possible.

Do people describe and experience eating disorders in the same way, everywhere?

Though there is more in common than not in how people experience eating disorders, the expression of symptoms does occur within a social context. In medieval Europe, for example, fasting was viewed as a form of asceticism and a means toward salvation. Accounts of holy anorexia suggest that the core feature of anorexia nervosa—severely restricted intake together with a reluctance to eat despite dangerously low weights—was thought to bring one closer to God.

Recent research across different cultures tells us that in non-Western cultures, symptoms of eating disorders are more commonly expressed in terms of physical symptoms rather than as exaggerated concerns about body image. A non–fat-phobic version of anorexia nervosa has been well documented in China, Japan, Singapore, and India and in Asian communities within the United States. Someone with this version of anorexia nervosa may describe a culturally relevant reason for restrictive eating and failure to maintain normal weight, such as feeling too full or having a vaguely upset stomach. The distress associated with bulimic symptoms may also vary cross-culturally, with some early research suggesting that binge eating causes more distress for Caucasians, African Americans, and Latinos, whereas vomiting causes more distress for Asians.

Within Western cultures, the language that gets associated with eating disorder symptoms can be closely related to a particular subculture as well. Athletes in sports such as wrestling, ballet, cross country running, weight lifting, and gymnastics may talk about disordered behaviors like restrictive eating, use of laxatives or supplements, and frequent weighing in terms of performance enhancement (rather than concern about being fat or one's overall appearance). But these behaviors still pose a threat to emotional and physical well-being. Weight and fitness expectations for members of the military can present a similar risk.

Another group of individuals who sometimes describe eating disorder symptoms uniquely are boys and men. One key distinguishing feature in this population is the nature of the body dissatisfaction underlying abnormal behaviors. Men tend to focus on form (i.e., leanness or muscularity) and function (i.e., actual or perceived difficulty with physical performance) rather than other aspects of appearance such as thinness or weight.

While we have outlined ways people have differed in their descriptions of eating disorder symptoms across the ages, sexes, and different cultures, we are compelled to end with a reminder that, once entrenched as an illness, the descriptions and manifestations of disturbances in thinking and behavior across these groups are far more similar than different.

Focusing on: The facts

Eating disorders involve disturbances in eating and eating-related behaviors. In addition to their impact on psychological well-being and day-to-day functioning, they are associated with significant risks to physical health, including heart function, fertility, and bone and dental health.

In the United States, eating disorder diagnoses are outlined in a guidebook called the DSM-5, which provides links to a worldwide classification system, the ICD-10.

Anorexia nervosa, bulimia nervosa, and binge-eating disorder are the best defined and well-understood eating disorders. Pica, rumination disorder, and ARFID were, in the past, included in a section of the DSM called "feeding disorders" and less is known about them. DSM-5 describes a set of other feeding and eating disorders as well. These are concerning conditions because they also pose threats to psychological and physical health, but additional research is needed to understand how best to define them, what their typical features are, and how best to treat them. Obesity is not an eating disorder.

Eating disorders sit on one end of a continuum. On the other end is normal eating, which is characterized by flexibility and balance. Disordered eating sits somewhere in the middle, and the range of eating behaviors and attitudes about food, body shape, and weight that might be considered disordered is very diverse.

2

WHO GETS EATING DISORDERS?

There is a lot of misinformation about who develops eating disorders. At least in part, owing to inaccurate assumptions about who can and who cannot experience these disorders, nearly half of individuals with an eating problem do not receive specialty treatment for their symptoms. The problem is apparent on both sides of the treatment-seeking equation—with healthcare providers and with patients. For example, mental health professionals may be less likely to recognize and refer non-white people for treatment, and in the United States, eating disorder services are used less frequently by African Americans, Latino Americans, and Asian Americans than by white, non-Hispanic populations. Thus, it is crucial that we set the record straight on who can develop an eating disorder—namely, anyone; no one is immune.

How widespread are eating disorders?

Despite all the publicity it receives, anorexia nervosa has always been and remains a relatively uncommon disorder. The best information currently available indicates that about 1% of women in the United States will develop anorexia nervosa over the course of their lives. Men also develop anorexia nervosa, but much less frequently; somewhere between 0.1 and 0.5% of men in the United States will develop anorexia nervosa. Bulimia nervosa is more common. One to two percent of women and 0.5% of men in the United States will develop this eating disorder over the course of their lives.

We should underscore that these are rough estimates and likely to be on the low side. Studies of relatively uncommon conditions such as anorexia nervosa and bulimia nervosa are challenging. For example, in one study of 1,000 women, if the rate of anorexia nervosa is 1%, only 10 women would be expected to have it. Missing just a few others who are affected would lead to a significant underestimate. In addition, the nature of these eating disorders likely leads to underestimates. Individuals with anorexia nervosa typically play down their symptoms or simply do not believe they have a problem. Therefore, they may not be counted in a survey that asks respondents whether they have problems with their eating or weight. Similarly, individuals with bulimia nervosa are usually embarrassed about their binge eating and purging, and they may not admit to engaging in such behavior when asked. Therefore, even the best surveys we have likely underestimate the number of people with anorexia nervosa and bulimia nervosa.

The most recently recognized eating disorder, binge-eating disorder, is more common than anorexia nervosa or bulimia nervosa and affects 2–3% of adults in the United States over the course of their lives (3–4% of women, 2% of men). Surprisingly, even though this disorder may begin during adolescence, individuals with binge-eating disorder tend to present for treatment at an older age than do those with anorexia nervosa and bulimia nervosa.

Are there really only a handful of eating disorders?

Full-fledged definitions are available for only six eating disorders: anorexia nervosa, bulimia nervosa, binge-eating disorder, avoidant/restrictive food intake disorder (ARFID), pica, and rumination disorder. This is because healthcare providers and researchers have seen considerable numbers of patients with these problems over the years, so much so that there is substantial knowledge about what they are. That is why these six disorders are described in some detail in the fifth edition of the *Diagnostic and Statistical Manual of Mental Disorders* (DSM-5). As previously described, the DSM-5, published by the American Psychiatric Association, is a widely used reference outlining the defining characteristics of all mental disorders.

Two of the authors of this book were part of the committee that put together the eating disorders section of DSM-5, and it's important to acknowledge that we and our colleagues recognize that some individuals suffer from significant eating problems that do not meet the criteria for one of these six disorders. For example, some individuals self-induce vomiting, not after a binge meal as do individuals with bulimia nervosa, but after eating a perfectly normal amount of food. Other individuals who were once overweight or obese lose a substantial amount of weight and develop many of the psychological and physical features of anorexia nervosa but never become underweight by the usual standards. Those who specialize in the treatment of eating disorders are familiar with individuals with these sorts of problems, but not enough is known yet for us to clearly define and fully characterize them. In the DSM-5 system, these problems fall into a category called *other specified feeding and eating disorders* (OSFED). Detailed descriptions of OSFED can be found in Chapter 1.

The best available information suggests that disordered eating, a broad term that describes a range of problematic behaviors, including those that would fall into the OSFED category, is much more common than the disorders fully recognized in DSM-5. In other words, disturbed eating behaviors, whether part of a full-fledged eating disorder or not, are a very frequent source of distress and impairment. Estimates of the frequency of disordered eating vary, in part because of different definitions of what constitutes disordered eating. However, it is likely that at least 10% of young people in the United States suffer from some form of a broadly defined eating disorder.

Are minority populations immune from getting eating disorders?

We do not know with certainty the frequencies of specific eating disorders across all racial and ethnic groups in the United States, much less across the globe. However, it is certain that no racial or ethnic group is immune: Each of the six formally defined eating disorders has been described among individuals of all racial and ethnic groups.

There are hints that different ethnic groups may be more or less vulnerable to developing specific disorders. It appears that anorexia nervosa occurs less frequently among African Americans and that binge eating may be somewhat more common among Latino Americans. It must be emphasized that these are tentative findings rather than established facts, but they suggest that sociocultural influences may impact vulnerability across different racial and ethnic groups.

Is this only a problem for teenagers?

Sometimes people assume that eating disorders are really only a problem for teenagers and young adults. It is true that adolescence is a developmental transition period and a risky time for the onset of eating problems; the peak age of the first presentation of anorexia nervosa and bulimia nervosa is between 15 and 25 years old. Nonetheless, it is possible to develop and continue to experience an eating disorder as an adult. Most individuals with binge-eating disorder are in their 30s or 40s when they first obtain treatment. Furthermore, some individuals who develop anorexia nervosa, bulimia nervosa, or ARFID while young never conquer the problem and therefore continue to suffer with the problem as adults.

In the United States, eating disorders affect around 3.5% of women and 1–2% of men over age 40, with binge-eating disorder and OSFED being the most common eating disorders among older individuals. For some women, the transition of menopause appears, like puberty, to be a critical period of risk for eating disorders.

Eating disorders can also occur during childhood. In fact, childhood is the typical age of onset of pica, rumination, and ARFID. And, rarely, anorexia nervosa and bulimia nervosa develop before puberty. This means that disordered eating and eating disorders occur in both women and men of all ages.

Is this only a problem for the wealthy?

Within the United States, eating disorders are broadly distributed across socioeconomic categories, meaning that these disorders are far from reserved for the wealthy. Since 1990, with recent support from the Bill and Melinda Gates Foundation, the Global Burden of Disease Study has assessed the impact of a range of health conditions, and in 2010 anorexia nervosa and bulimia nervosa were added to the conditions whose impacts were assessed. Of 306 physical and mental disorders, these eating disorders ranked as the 12th-leading contributor to health burden in high-income countries and 46th in low- and middle-income countries. In addition, a recent study in the United States found that, among low-income individuals relying on food pantries, those with the highest levels of food insecurity had the highest rates of binge eating. Such information underscores the fact that eating disorders have an impact across the wealth spectrum.

How is the development of eating disorders affected by culture?

Eating disorders have long been viewed as culture-bound to Western traditions and thus have been increasingly well identified and classified in North America, Europe, Australia, and New Zealand. However, the twenty-first century has brought with it the understanding that these devastating illnesses are, unfortunately, an equal-opportunity problem, occurring in non-Western cultures as well.

For some eating disorders, the transmission of Western ideals (e.g., equating thinness with beauty) and economic factors (e.g., an abundance of food available for binge eating) may play an important role in their development among people from non-Western cultures. In Fiji, for example, global economic and cultural advancement, urban migration, and changes in social norms for appearance (in part due to the arrival of television, Western magazines, and, later, the Internet) set the stage for girls and women to more commonly worry about eating, body shape, dietary restriction, and obesity than previously.

Although eating disorders have been described across cultures, their frequency and manifestations have not yet been well examined in non-Western cultures. Misclassification may result from differences in the symptoms of eating disorders in different parts of the world. One cultural variation of anorexia nervosa, for example, is the absence of fat phobia among some individuals who otherwise meet diagnostic criteria for the disorder. As mentioned in Chapter 1, rather than describing an intense fear of gaining weight and becoming fat, individuals in Asia and India appear more likely to complain of vague physical discomfort that prevents them from eating. And in Fiji, a difference in the reasoning behind the use of traditional herbs, a normal, culturally consistent behavior, may greatly matter; for adolescent girls who have become exposed to Western ideals of attractiveness, using these herbs for the express purpose of weight management may signal emotional distress frequently seen with an eating disorder, such as being overly concerned with eating, body shape, or weight. On the other hand, symptoms such as an intense preoccupation with food have been mistakenly interpreted as a symptom of an eating disorder among people who cannot get enough to eat because of poverty and shortage of resources.

Are there people who are especially at risk for developing an eating disorder?

Though we will soon make the point that eating disorders do affect boys and men, current research continues to indicate that being female puts people at greater risk for developing this type of problem.

Experiencing a significant stressor—be it an expected developmental and biological transition such as puberty or an unexpected event such as the loss of a parent—also adds risk for the development of an eating disorder. And, as one would expect intuitively, the more stressors, the higher the risk.

In addition, certain personality traits appear to increase the chances of developing an eating disorder. The most recent science suggests that perfectionistic traits—liking things to be neat and tidy, being especially careful to do things properly—predispose some individuals to the development of anorexia nervosa. However, obsessional traits are, for most individuals, extremely helpful in grappling with the complex world in which we live. And most teenage girls with perfectionist traits will never develop anorexia nervosa. People who develop bulimia nervosa and binge-eating disorder are somewhat more prone to problems having to do with impulse control, such as substance abuse or conduct problems, prior to developing an eating disorder.

Some individuals who develop eating disorders experience significant symptoms of anxiety or depression during childhood. While additional research is needed for definitive answers, the presence of generalized anxiety disorder, social phobia, or obsessive-compulsive disorder during childhood appears to add to the risk for developing anorexia nervosa. Persistent mood symptoms—such as low mood, lack of interest in pleasurable activities, and guilt—seem to increase risk for development of anorexia or bulimia nervosa. Again, these findings should be interpreted with care, as (1) most youngsters who experience anxiety or depression do not go on to develop eating disorders, and (2) the presence of childhood anxiety or depression may be as likely to lead to alternate mental health problems in adulthood as an eating problem.

Are boys and men immune from developing eating disorders?

No. It is true that more women than men are affected by eating disorders, as is also the case for many anxiety and mood disorders. However, recent US surveys of the lifetime frequency of eating disorders tell us that binge-eating disorder is almost as common in men as in women, and that men represent 10–20% of the cases of anorexia and bulimia nervosa.

In addition, it is possible that eating disorders among boys and men are more frequently overlooked than among women. Misidentification of eating disorders can occur for a variety of reasons. In the case of anorexia nervosa, for example, revisions in the description of the diagnosis for DSM-5 include the removal of the diagnostic criterion about disruptions in menstrual functioning, which might have caused clinicians to dismiss the diagnosis for boys and men. Criteria aside, the questions we ask people about their symptoms also matter. While placing a high degree of importance on body shape and weight is a well-known feature of eating disorders, this is typically assessed by mental health providers using concepts like a fear of weight gain or a drive for thinness. In boys and men, however, research suggests that the ideal male body is characterized by a dual focus on muscularity and leanness (i.e., low body fat). It is possible that the myth that boys and men do not get eating disorders has in part been perpetuated by flaws in our assessment.

Equally if not more important, boys and men are no more protected from the cycle of an eating disorder than they are from developing one. The vulnerable male's pathway into disordered eating and an eating disorder may, in some cases,

differ from the vulnerable female's. Yet, once entrenched in behaviors of illness—following rigid food rules, obsessing about
body shape and weight, engaging in compensatory actions—
the course of eating disorders and the associated distress are
far more similar than different across the sexes.

Are eating disorders on the rise?

There is little doubt that the last 50 years have witnessed a substantial increase in recommendations from medical experts to
eat healthy. Equally certain is the significant decrease in the
body weights of female models who appear in popular media
and of beauty contest winners. It seems logical to imagine that
these cultural influences would lead to a rise in the frequency
of eating disorders.

Remarkably, that does not appear to have happened! The
best information from the United States and Europe indicates
that the frequency of anorexia nervosa is stable and that the
frequency of bulimia nervosa has actually *declined*. Because
binge-eating disorder and ARFID are relatively newer diagnoses, we do not yet have information about trends in their
prevalence over time.

Research from around the world tells us that the health
burdens associated with these problems are increasing,
underscoring how much trouble they can cause and that
they are likely on the rise in low- and middle-income countries. This may be attributed to a number of factors alluded to
throughout this chapter. These include the improved identification of cases, an increasingly dynamic global economy that
allows for widespread exposure to products originating in the
West (including inexpensive, high-calorie, palatable foods),
and an expansion of communication platforms such as social
media (through which ideas, messages, and images that, for
vulnerable individuals, compound the risk of developing an
eating disorder can quickly spread).

Focusing on: The frequency of eating disorders

There is much misinformation about how common eating disorders are and about who develops them, but here is what we actually know.

Anorexia nervosa affects approximately 1% of women and about one-tenth as many men in the United States. Two percent of women and 0.5% of men will develop bulimia nervosa in their lifetime. The best information from the United States and Europe suggests that the frequency of anorexia nervosa is stable but that the frequency of bulimia nervosa has actually declined significantly in recent years. Binge-eating disorder is more common than anorexia nervosa or bulimia nervosa and affects 3–4% of women and 2% of men in the United States over the course of their lives. Estimates of the frequency of disordered eating vary greatly, in part because of different definitions of what constitutes disordered eating. However, it is likely that at least 10% of young people in the United States suffer from some form of a broadly defined eating disorder, including OSFED.

No one is immune from developing an eating disorder. They are seen in people of all races, ethnicities, and ages and of any socioeconomic status. However, virtually all research suggests that women are at greater risk than men.

While eating disorders have been described across many cultures, their frequency and manifestations in non-Western cultures require further study and documentation. More research is also needed into what factors predispose some people to developing eating disorders.

3

HOW DO YOU KNOW IF YOU OR SOMEONE YOU CARE ABOUT HAS AN EATING DISORDER?

Unfortunately, eating disorders are sometimes easier to recognize in someone else than in oneself. They often develop innocently as someone tries to cut out unhealthy foods or lose a few pounds because a friend was doing the same. Or maybe a coach at school mentioned that a runner's cross country racing time might improve if they lost a bit of weight. Dietary changes and even modest weight loss do not indicate the presence of an eating disorder. Instead, an eating disorder means that these behaviors have become routine and are causing significant trouble. It becomes hard to imagine living life without them. Thoughts about body shape and weight are constantly intruding and feel inescapable. Fear of weight gain is frequent, even if one's weight is normal or low. People with eating disorders develop rules about foods, and ideas about food become all-or-nothing and extreme. For example, people with eating disorders often come to believe that certain foods are "good" and others "bad," or that if dietary rules are not strictly observed, then loss of control of eating is inevitable or that compensatory behaviors such as exercise or self-induced vomiting are necessary.

When should you or someone you care about be evaluated?

If and when you become concerned about a preoccupation with food or that eating behaviors include new and unhealthy patterns, you may want to ask your primary care provider whether an eating disorder is present, or you may want to be evaluated by an eating disorder specialist. To find an eating disorder specialist in your local area, you can ask your current healthcare provider or your insurance company, or consult national professional organizations with referral resources (outlined in the Resources section of this book), including those available through the National Eating Disorders Association (NEDA) (https://www.nationaleatingdisorders.org/) and Academy for Eating Disorders (AED) (https://www.aedweb.org).

Sometimes, the motivation for treatment stems from how much time or mental real estate is being taken up by eating, avoiding eating, or thinking about food, eating, and appearance. Sometimes the motivation for treatment comes from a growing awareness that normal routines have been disrupted—for example, no longer eating with the family—or from worries about the impact of behavior on others—for example, concern that a child may be influenced by a parent's inability to eat normally at family mealtimes. In general, it is a good sign if someone recognizes the need for help for an eating problem or eating disorder.

The more difficult question may be when, and how, to help someone else. Often it is useful to think about whether a significant change has occurred in the eating behaviors, weight, or social interactions of the person you're worrying about. An evaluation is appropriate when weight is unhealthy—either too low or too high—and when the current weight is different from the person's normal baseline. An evaluation is also called for when someone

- has dramatically changed the foods eaten,
- is no longer eating favorite foods or is following strict food rules, or

- is eating in patterns that appear unusual—consuming large amounts of food followed by frequent trips to the bathroom, for instance, or eating only vegetables rather than items from a range of food groups.

Finally, an evaluation is appropriate when someone's social life is changing because of the suffering experienced around eating (see Table 3.1).

Though it can be difficult to figure out what to say to someone whose behavior or health is worrisome, it is important to say something if you are concerned about possible eating disorder symptoms. Specific concerns—observable changes in behavior, mood or attitude about eating, or weight

Table 3.1. Common signs of social difficulties around eating in eating disorders

	Examples
At Home	• Refusing to eat in front of family • Eating different foods than what has been prepared for a family meal • Refusing to eat foods prepared by another family member • Eating in one's room • Eating in secret
At Work	• Eating very little or nothing at work functions • Difficulty participating in meetings or social gatherings due to anxiety and/or guilt about eating • Refusing to join colleagues for lunch
At School	• Skipping opportunities to eat with friends at or after school • Refusing to eat any food provided by the school cafeteria
Across Situations	• Avoiding meals in social settings because of having "just eaten," or "will be eating later" • Trouble participating in conversations at mealtime due to anxiety and/or guilt about eating or preoccupations about food • Difficulty ordering flexibly and eating adequately when sharing foods with others (i.e., eating "family style")

or appearance—can be shared in private and in a supportive tone. In our experience, exactly what to say will likely depend on the nature of the relationship between the individuals involved. While there is no perfect thing to say, here are a few examples:

- "I'm worried about you. I notice that you seem nervous when a group of us are eating together, and that you leave to use the bathroom during the meal sometimes. Is everything OK?"
- "Are you feeling alright? You don't look well."
- "I have heard you talking a lot about being unhappy with how you look. I care about you and I am wondering how you are feeling. Maybe talking to someone about this might help you feel better."

If you suggest that the person speak with someone who can offer a professional opinion, you can offer to help them figure out the best next steps. If the conversation feels tense, if the person does not acknowledge the problem, or if you do not have an especially close relationship with the person, another option is for you to simply make yourself available as someone to talk to when they are ready. When the person whose health is a concern is a child, teen, or young adult, sharing worries with a member of that person's family may be appropriate.

Who evaluates people for eating disorders?

Eating disorders are conditions that affect both physical and emotional health. As a result, they are often evaluated and treated by medical professionals as well as by mental health professionals.

For children and adolescents, pediatricians and adolescent medicine specialists are generally in an excellent position to assess the initial signs of a possible problem. These providers are used to tracking weight, growth, and general nutritional health, and many of them have questions about eating and exercise already included in their routine evaluations. They will know how to ask additional questions when a family member expresses concern about a possible eating disorder.

Primary care providers who see adult patients vary a lot in how much experience they have in evaluating individuals with eating disorders. Mental health clinicians, including psychiatrists, psychologists, and social workers, may have more experience with individuals who may have an eating disorder, and at least one of these professionals will usually be involved in a treatment plan for an adult patient with a known eating disorder. Some clinicians identify themselves as specialists in eating disorders. This does not have a specific meaning in terms of the training or ability of the clinician; rather, it may mean that the clinician has an interest in or experience with this area of specialty, or they may be associated with an eating disorder treatment program.

What is the evaluation process like? Are there tests that prove that someone has an eating disorder?

There is no one test that proves that someone has, or does not have, an eating disorder. The evaluation process may vary for different individuals, but it will always include a conversation with a clinician. Whether the evaluation takes place with a medical doctor or a mental health provider, there will be questions about thoughts and feelings about food, weight, and body shape. Individuals undergoing an evaluation may be asked to complete a diagnostic screening tool, either a questionnaire or interview with a standard set of questions, such as the Eating Attitudes Test (EAT-26, available free online at https://www.eat-26.com/) or the Eating Disorders Assessment for DSM-5 eating disorders (EDA-5, accessible via https://eda5.org/). Regardless of the evaluation's format, there should be discussions about eating behavior, and there may be specific questions about what someone has eaten recently. There should also be questions about weight history and about family history of eating and eating disorders. Girls and women will be asked about past and current menstrual functioning.

Because there is no specific test to prove the presence of an eating disorder, any evaluation relies on the accuracy (and honesty) of the person being evaluated. Healthcare providers with experience in treating eating disorders are well aware that this may be a limitation and are generally skilled in asking questions that are most likely to elicit meaningful answers, even when people find it difficult to discuss their symptoms.

Clinicians also may look for physical signs of an eating disorder. In addition to measuring a person's weight (and not simply assuming the patient's reported weight is accurate), they may look for signs of possible illness, such as body-checking (i.e., a pattern of touching, pinching, or measuring body parts, including one's wrists, ribs, hip bone, etc.), visible dental erosion, or calluses on the back of the hand resulting from repeatedly using it to self-induce vomiting. Commonly, an evaluation for an eating disorder includes a physical assessment, such as a physical exam (with attention to vital signs such as heart rate, blood pressure, and temperature), an electrocardiogram, and blood tests (with attention to serum electrolytes such as sodium and potassium) and blood cell counts (including red and white blood cells). These physical assessments are not the same as a test for an eating disorder, but they may provide supportive evidence that an eating disorder is present and information about how seriously it has affected the body.

What other conditions resemble eating disorders?

Eating disorders may resemble other illnesses that affect eating, weight, or both. For anorexia nervosa, an illness identified by its significantly low weight, illnesses such as cancer,

HIV, hyperthyroidism, and other conditions may be considered during the evaluation process. Anorexia nervosa can be easily distinguished from these medical conditions because there are specific medical tests available that can confirm the presence of a cancer or an infection such as HIV.

Similarly, binge-eating disorder may be difficult to diagnose in the context of a medical condition that increases appetite. For example, hormone disturbances such as Cushing's disease or insulin-dependent diabetes may lead to overeating, chaotic eating, or other eating disturbances that may appear similar to the eating pattern typical of binge-eating disorder.

Sometimes individuals with eating disorders see a clinician, having become convinced that they have a medical problem other than an eating disorder. The patient or the patient's family may be concerned about one or more of the nonspecific gastrointestinal problems associated with eating disorders and believe, for example, that fullness or bloating is due to a medical problem or a food allergy, not an eating disorder. The evaluation in this case may include assessments to rule out certain medical problems, and ultimately to educate the patient, family, or both about medical changes, such as changes to the gastrointestinal system, that take place when an eating disorder is present.

Sometimes the evaluation requires distinguishing one eating disorder from another. For example, an individual may present with complaints about binge-eating episodes and may not disclose self-induced vomiting behavior. The clinician may need to distinguish binge-eating disorder (frequent episodes of out-of-control binge eating) from bulimia nervosa (binge-eating episodes together with inappropriate compensatory behaviors such as self-induced vomiting or laxative misuse). As another example, someone with low weight may require an evaluation that distinguishes whether they are affected by anorexia nervosa or avoidant/restrictive food intake disorder (ARFID; characterized by avoidant or restrictive eating that is not due to concern about body shape or weight).

Eating disorders also need to be distinguished from other problems that may have similar symptoms. For example, individuals with social anxiety disorder may avoid all social occasions because they fear interaction with others, whereas individuals with ARFID avoid social occasions because they fear they will be expected to eat foods that they are not comfortable consuming. There is substantial overlap in the symptoms of these two disorders, but the focus of treatment should differ— the treatment of ARFID promotes eating a broader variety of foods, while the treatment of social anxiety disorder focuses on developing a broader range of interactions with others.

What other conditions may occur together with eating disorders?

Eating disorders may occur together with certain other psychiatric disorders, the most common of which are depression and anxiety disorders. It can be hard to know whether an upset mood and anxious feelings that may accompany an eating disorder meet criteria for a separate diagnosis, so any complete evaluation will need to include questions about emotional health from before the onset of the eating disorder, as well as close monitoring for a period of time after the initial evaluation in order to determine with more certainty whether a separate condition is present. Anorexia nervosa can co-occur with obsessive-compulsive disorder (OCD), and some of the eating disorders co-occur with substance use disorders.

In addition to psychiatric conditions that may be present alongside eating disorders, there may be medical conditions that occur in association with eating disorders. Some of the medical complications of eating disorders, such as poor bone health or osteoporosis in anorexia nervosa, or inflammation of the esophagus (esophagitis) in bulimia nervosa, may develop into a situation where a patient must manage two related conditions at one time. Some medical conditions that develop together with an eating disorder will resolve when the eating disorder resolves. This is the case with esophagitis in bulimia nervosa, or the slowed stomach emptying and constipation seen in anorexia nervosa and bulimia nervosa. Some conditions do not reverse with treatment of the eating disorder. This may be the case with osteoporosis associated with anorexia nervosa, and with dental erosion associated with bulimia nervosa.

Focusing on: Identification of the problem

Eating disorders can be easier to recognize in other people. If the signs of an eating disorder are apparent in someone else— such as changes in eating behavior or weight, or worrisome attitudes about food, exercise, or appearance—it is important to say something to the person. If one is concerned about changes in one's own emotional and/or physical health related to eating and related behaviors, seeking out a medical or mental health clinician for an evaluation is essential.

Clinicians will ask a range of questions to assess the presence of an eating disorder, and the accuracy of the diagnosis and helpfulness of the treatment plan will rely on honest responses to sometimes difficult questions. A physical examination and blood tests are likely to be part of a comprehensive evaluation. The mental health and physical health assessment are both designed to determine the presence of other emotional or physiological problems that might affect the treatment recommended. As a number of wide-ranging symptoms—from anxiety to mood to gastrointestinal functioning—can develop in association with an eating disorder, treatment of the eating problem may provide relief to a variety of symptoms, including those seemingly unrelated to the eating disorder. But, depending on the nature of the co-occurring problem, additional treatment may be warranted.

4

WHAT CAUSES EATING DISORDERS?

Eating disorders are complex illnesses, associated with problems in emotions, behavior, and medical well-being. For many illnesses, the most effective treatments have come as a result of identifying the cause—for example, effective treatment for AIDS became possible only after a specific virus (HIV) was established to be the cause. Therefore, much healthcare research is devoted to understanding the causes of illnesses. Unfortunately, unlike infections like AIDS, complex psychiatric disorders, including eating disorders, appear to have multiple complicated causes.

What do genes have to do with it?

Contained in the DNA we inherit from our parents, genes contribute in important ways to who we are. Genes play a major role in determining our height, our intelligence, and our eye color. Some human characteristics are determined entirely by genes. For example, blood type—whether your blood is type A, type B, type AB, or type O—is controlled by a single gene. Other characteristics, like hair color, are completely determined genetically but by contributions from multiple genes.

Genes also contribute importantly to our vulnerability to many illnesses, including asthma, diabetes, and high blood pressure. But, for these and most illnesses, many, many genes make contributions—some increasing risk and some decreasing it—and the influence of genes interacts with the influence of environment. In other words, it's complicated. And, for most common human illnesses, even though genes play a role in determining vulnerability, they do not strictly determine who will get sick and who will not.

This is also true of most mental disorders, including eating disorders. It has been known for many years that eating disorders such as anorexia nervosa tend to run in families. If one girl in a family has had anorexia nervosa, it is more likely than average that a sister will develop it; however, most of the time, the sister does not. It has now been well established that some of the risk for developing eating disorders is genetic, and this contributes to their running in families. However, there is no evidence that a single gene is responsible, and most researchers believe that multiple genes interact in very complicated ways (that we do not yet well understand) with the environment to increase risk. For example, a culture that, for women, equates being thin with being attractive likely adds an environmental risk to an individual's own genetic risk for developing an eating disorder. For more information on the latest research in genetics and eating disorders, see Chapter 18.

Is it anyone's fault?

When something unfortunate happens, we tend to look for something or someone to blame. This is true even when the unfortunate event is an illness and the ultimate cause (or, more commonly, causes) is not known.

Yet, there is no single cause for the development of an eating disorder. Therefore, an eating disorder is no one person's fault. Many factors appear to contribute to eating disorders, including genes, personal characteristics, age, and the environment. Attempts to decide who is at fault are no more appropriate when someone develops an eating disorder than when someone develops asthma. The crucial issue is not "Who is to blame?" but "What can we do?"

Can eating disorders be prevented?

The ultimate cure for a disease is to prevent it from occurring in the first place. For a very few illnesses, this has been achieved, smallpox probably being the best example. A vaccine against the virus that causes smallpox became available in the early 1800s, and over the succeeding century and a half, universal vaccination (i.e., everyone being vaccinated) was eventually implemented across the globe. By 1980, the World Health Organization certified that smallpox had been eradicated, eliminating the need for vaccinations.

The smallpox example is illustrative because it highlights that complete prevention is easiest when an illness has a single, known cause. Unfortunately, this is not the case for most illnesses, including eating disorders. Therefore, researchers instead focus on identifying risk factors for an illness and reducing these, figuring that reduction of risk will lead to a reduction in the frequency of illness. This approach has been successfully applied to heart disease. Over the last 50 years in the United States, there has been a major public health effort to reduce risk factors for heart disease, such as smoking, high blood pressure, and insufficient exercise, leading to a marked decline in the number of deaths due to heart disease.

In recent years, similar prevention-based approaches have been developed for eating disorders (two examples are programs known as the Body Project and StudentBodies), with growing evidence of their effectiveness. These programs aim to reduce the idealization of thinness, especially among girls and young women, and have been utilized in middle and high schools and college campuses, including sororities. And while we don't know exactly why people develop eating disorders, the good news is that these prevention programs seem to work, reducing some risk factors for and symptoms of eating disorders. Benefits appear strongest for reducing binge eating and other symptoms of bulimia nervosa; the prevention of anorexia nervosa remains more problematic.

There is a strong consensus that, in addition to reducing risk factors, it is critical to intervene as soon as possible when individuals begin to show or experience clear symptoms, a tactic termed *secondary prevention*.

What are some risk factors for eating disorders?

Many factors contribute to the risk of developing an eating disorder, including the following:

- Being female
- Some genes a person inherits from their parents
- Living in a culture that emphasizes the value of being thin
- An inborn tendency to be anxious and depressed
- Puberty
- Experiencing a stressful life event
- Going on a diet

But, some people with *all* of these characteristics will never develop an eating disorder. The cause appears to be a complicated interaction between these and other factors that have still not been identified.

Are they caused by dieting?

There is little doubt that dieting (that is, attempting to reduce one's intake of calories) is involved in important ways in the development and persistence of eating disorders. Most people who develop an eating disorder say that they were attempting to diet when they first developed symptoms of the eating disorder. In anorexia nervosa, restriction of caloric intake is a defining characteristic. And, although the key behaviors of bulimia nervosa and subthreshold bulimia nervosa (considered an OSFED) are binge eating and inappropriate attempts to compensate for binge eating (such as inducing vomiting), individuals with bulimia nervosa usually diet between episodes of binge eating. It is unclear to what degree people with purging disorder pursue rigorous dieting.

The question of causation is trickier. For example, the overwhelming majority of American teenage girls diet at some point. But only a small minority of them develop an eating disorder. If eating disorders were simply caused by dieting, they would be much more common than they are. Similarly, although the frequency of dieting among young people has likely increased in the last 50 years, our best estimates tell us that the frequency of anorexia nervosa has not, and the frequency of bulimia nervosa has probably declined. For these reasons, dieting is best viewed as one of a number of risk factors for the development of eating disorders, but not as the cause. For people who have additional but unclear vulnerabilities, dieting triggers the development of symptoms that may evolve into an eating disorder.

Are they caused by families?

As discussed already, we do not know what causes eating disorders. Nonetheless, for many years, families were blamed. It is likely that this mistaken notion developed because when parents took their child to get help, the parents were in great distress. But as all parents can imagine, such distress is perfectly normal when a child has a serious illness, whether it's an eating disorder or a purely physical problem! Professionals likely misinterpreted the distress as indicating there was dysfunction in the family that had preceded the eating disorder and led to its development. This line of thinking has now been discarded.

Put simply: Since we do not know what causes eating disorders, we cannot blame the family.

Are they caused by the media?

The answer to this question is not simple. The images that the media presents of individuals, especially women, who are suggested to be attractive and popular are, almost without exception, much thinner (and younger) than the average person. This phenomenon contributes to the near-universal desire among young women to be thin (or at least thinner). For boys and men, the images in popular media suggest that attractiveness is linked to being muscular and buffed. So overall, there is good reason to believe that the images portrayed in the media contribute to unrealistic and unattainable ideals of what people should look like and, by extension, an environment in which eating disorders are more likely to develop.

But, this does not mean that the media alone has the power to cause eating disorders. In industrialized countries, young people are flooded with images in the media, but only a few of those exposed develop an eating disorder. Furthermore, eating disorders were clearly described long before the current media environment—the term *anorexia nervosa* was coined 150 years ago!

Are they caused by friends?

Most of what we know about the influence of peers on the development of eating disorders comes from studies of young people. During adolescence, separation from the family increases and attention (and time spent) shifts more and more to friends. Friendships made in these formative years can be influential well into the future. Longer-term studies have found that exposure to friends who are dieting predicts more body dissatisfaction, use of extreme and unhealthy weight-control behaviors, and loss-of-control eating five years later. On the other hand, friendships with people who do not overly value appearance or dieting may help protect a vulnerable teen from becoming too focused on thinness.

In studies of college students, a roommate's commitment to dieting has been found to predict an individual's drive for thinness, bulimic symptoms, and purging status. This impact can be lasting. Despite the shifts in social environments that are likely to occur over time, college roommate dieting is also associated with the likelihood of unhealthy weight-control behaviors for women in their 30s. Essentially, it seems that friends form a micro-environment that can add to or protect against eating-disordered attitudes and actions. Exactly how much (and by what mechanism) eating disturbances are contagious—particularly in shared living situations like dorms, apartments, or sorority or fraternity houses—remains unknown. So, like for other influences, we can conclude that peer influence is a factor, but not *the* factor, that might increase the chances of an eating disorder taking hold.

Focusing on: Causes

As is true for many or most of the illnesses that affect individuals in the modern world, there is no one, simple cause for eating disorders. Many risk factors, ranging from an individual's psychological makeup to the genes inherited from parents, media exposure, and peer influence, appear to play a role in increasing, and decreasing, the chances of developing an eating disorder. Therefore, it is a mistake to blame any single influence—be it a parent, a friend, or a TV show—for the development of an eating disorder. However, efforts to reduce exposure to unrealistic and unattainable images of attractiveness are worthwhile and important as a means of its prevention across the population.

5

WHAT COULD MAKE
AN EATING DISORDER
BETTER OR WORSE?

Since eating disorders are potentially so serious, it is important to consider what factors may make the problem better or worse. Often individuals with eating disorders may want to tackle only some parts of the illness. For example, someone who has episodes of binge eating and self-induced vomiting as well as intermittent food restriction may want treatment for the binge episodes but not for the other behaviors, believing that it is only the binge eating that is causing trouble. The treatment of an eating disorder, however, typically emphasizes the importance of normalizing *all* eating (and related) behavior, including eating three meals and a snack or two daily in order to normalize hunger cues, as well as creating a structure that helps limit time spent thinking about food and eating and decreases the risk of binge eating.

Eating disorders are complicated because some of the typical behaviors of illness are acceptable or even encouraged in people who do not have eating disorders. Whereas skipping a meal from time to time may be okay for a person without an eating disorder, doing so poses notable risk to someone with an eating disorder. Similarly, when considering whether someone should remain in a favorite dance class or participate in a 5K run for a favorite charity, the impact of the activity on a person's weight, overall health, food choices, and thoughts and feelings about body shape and weight should be taken into account.

Is it okay to exercise?

Exercise is healthy for most people, but it is much more complicated for someone with an eating disorder. Exercise serves various purposes. It may help mobility and balance, improve cardiovascular health, reduce stress, or assist strength or weight management. However, in the presence of an eating disorder, exercise tends primarily or exclusively to result from an intense drive to burn calories, to lose additional weight or prevent weight gain, and to maintain (rather than relieve) body dissatisfaction. Affected individuals may feel compelled to exercise, working out for long periods during the day, on most days every week. In this case, excessive physical activity may in and of itself be a symptom of an eating disorder.

For people with eating disorders, exercise can start to crowd out life. It may become difficult to interrupt exercise routines and to live up to expectations at work, at school, or in relationships if they interfere with exercise (see Table 5.1). For some people with an eating disorder, exercise targets aspects of physical appearance, such as abdominal muscles or flabbiness in the upper arm or other body area. This rationale for exercise may be more common among boys, men, or female athletes with eating disorders whose body-image issues may include emphasis on particular areas of body shape, leanness, or strength.

Questions about physical activity are typically part of any evaluation for an eating disorder, and tracking and/or changing aspects of physical activity may be part of a recovery plan (see Table 5.1). Exercise may be limited or even eliminated during some phases of treatment, especially if weight restoration is required and there is concern that exercise may make

Table 5.1. Signs of problematic exercise behavior and treatment interventions

Disordered Exercise Behavior	Treatment Intervention
Exercising while underweight	Discontinue informal exercise (e.g., always taking stairs, excessing walking). Discontinue formal exercise. Limit exercise to stretching, gentle yoga, meditation.
Exercising on a machine that counts the number of calories burned	Exercise without monitoring calories (e.g., outdoors, swimming, yoga, martial arts, exercise class).
Rigid exercise routine	Vary type of activity, duration of workout, and intensity of workout. Introduce informal exercise in lieu of formal exercise.
Exercising to target appearance of specific part of the body	Exercise with others. Vary type of activity. Avoid classes targeting specific body parts (e.g., abdominal exercise class).
Body-checking in mirror while exercising	Exercise without mirrors.
Daily exercise	Build in rest days.
Exercising to compensate for binge eating	Delay exercise, minimize intensity/duration of workout, exercise with others.

this more difficult. Commonly, treatment includes reintroduction of healthy exercise patterns, including stretching, strength training, and even cardio-strength exercises, done in moderation. When someone develops an eating disorder in the context of an athletic activity such as competitive running or ballet, the physicians and mental health professionals treating that person may consider whether returning to this activity poses significant risk of eating disorder relapse, or whether the activity can be re-entered within reasonable parameters.

Is it possible to get better without professional help?

Eating disorders are behavioral disturbances, and if someone who is affected by an eating disorder is aware of the problem and motivated to change, they may be able to decrease illness-related behaviors and move toward health without help from a specialist. Sometimes the improvements take place without much effort. For example, some individuals who have intermittent binge-eating or purging episodes may experience a decrease in these behaviors if their environment changes, such as by going on a business trip or leaving for vacation. Sometimes these are only short-term improvements, but sometimes they last. Also, people with eating disorders who are motivated to interrupt their behaviors of illness may use self-help books, other written material about the recovery process, or smartphone apps (see Resources and Chapter 13 for lists of these resources) to help themselves achieve change without professional help. Self-help approaches have been well studied, with good results, for binge-eating–type disorders. There is less promising evidence of their usefulness in treating anorexia nervosa, and they have not yet been studied in ARFID.

For younger patients, there is strong evidence that families can be tremendously effective at helping a child, teen, or even young adult with an eating disorder (or older adults who live at home). Many families achieve these changes by working with a specialist who helps them carry out a family-based treatment approach, and there is some evidence to suggest that parental involvement in treatment is even more critical than the patient's attendance at sessions! Also, some families accomplish these changes for their children without much or any professional help, despite the child's level of motivation for change. Regardless of a child's age, most family members—be they parents, siblings, or partners—have a role to play in supporting their loved one with an eating disorder. Adults with eating disorders sometimes choose to connect with peer support as well. In the field of eating disorders research, there is a growing interest in peer support and peer mentorship as strategies for helping people stay motivated toward healthier behavior; however, there is not yet strong evidence supporting the effectiveness of this approach. F.E.A.S.T. (Families Empowered and Supporting Treatment of Eating Disorders) and Project HEAL are two organizations that offer online and in-person peer support for parents, families, and affected individuals (see Resources for more information).

While it is certainly possible to get better without professional help, there is no question that professional help can be useful. When symptoms are not particularly severe, or when an illness has just begun to take hold, it is reasonable to try anything that feels useful, including self-help and other approaches. However, when symptoms persist, return after a brief remission, or only improve a bit in the first place, individuals should consider seeing a specialist with experience in treating eating disorders or a generalist healthcare provider if access to specialty care is limited. Total symptom resolution—(a cure!)—is possible, but the longer symptoms remain in place, the harder it is to change them.

One of the tricky things about eating disorders is that they may bring on ambivalent feelings about health and well-being. People with anorexia nervosa, for example, are often reluctant to restore weight to normal because they fear weight gain and worry excessively about body shape and size. As a result, someone with anorexia nervosa may read this book and think that they do not need professional help, preferring instead to read a self-help book, or change their environment and improve their symptoms without doing anything else. All individuals with eating disorders, and family members who love them, need to remember that eating disorders are treatable illnesses, that symptoms of the illness can cloud judgment about the need for treatment, and that treatment delay may make full recovery more difficult. If one approach, including one that excludes professional help, is not effective, it is important to change to a new approach, perhaps increasing treatment intensity, and not to postpone changing course.

Why not use liposuction or other cosmetic surgery to change appearance?

Sometimes, people with eating disorders are so dissatisfied with the appearance of their bodies or of a specific body part that they become interested in the quick fix of cosmetic surgery to tuck their tummy, create a thigh gap, or remove fat via liposuction. While many cosmetic surgery procedures are approved by the US Food and Drug Administration (FDA) and may therefore seem safe enough, they may be particularly complicated for an individual with an eating disorder.

People with eating disorders worry a lot about their body shape and weight and have ideas that a change to the body (e.g., less fat, more muscle, more bony protuberances, etc.) will lead to feeling better in some way. These ideas are part of the illness fabric and are not reflective of reality. In other words, the idea that life will be better at a lower weight or with flatter or more toned abs is not actually true. In fact, studies that examine body satisfaction consistently find that, among individuals with eating disorders, body satisfaction does not improve with weight reduction and may actually worsen. Disordered beliefs respond best to specific types of talk therapy (outlined in Chapter 12) that address these problematic assumptions, not a surgical procedure. It's not a quick fix, but it is a more secure route to feeling better.

Of course, it's really hard for people to withstand the body dissatisfaction present during the active phases of most eating disorders. Some will describe these feelings as intolerable and the very worst part of what afflicts them. And frequently, body acceptance is the last phase of improvement in the treatment of an eating disorder. The belief that one's body is acceptable may only set in months or years after weight and eating behaviors have normalized. Nevertheless, cosmetic surgery is not a recommended treatment for fat phobia or other symptoms of illness, as it will not lead to lasting improvements in body image or self-esteem more broadly.

How does the use of social media affect eating disorder symptoms?

Social media is a reality of our lives, and many individuals with and without eating disorders use social media to communicate with friends and acquaintances. The problem is that for some, images of themselves or of their friends add to the worry about appearance and obsession with body shape and weight. People with eating disorders may feel competitive about their appearance, comparing current pictures of themselves with others from the past, or comparing themselves to their friends. Degree of engagement in photo-related activities, such as posting and sharing photos on Facebook or Instagram, is associated with body dissatisfaction and disordered eating. Several studies suggest that overall time spent looking at social media sites may decrease body acceptance or increase body-shape preoccupation. For adolescent girls, in particular, it appears that time spent on social media directly relates to internalizing the idea that thin is ideal, being driven to pursue thinness (sometimes at great cost), and scrutinizing the body closely in unhelpful ways (commonly referred to as a *body-checking*).

Individuals with eating disorders should discuss with their treatment providers whether spending time on social media is upsetting to them. Talking about social media experiences in detail is an important element of getting help in treatment; if the reply to a question about social media use is something like "Sure, I use Instagram," there is definitely more worth saying! For some people, following social media profiles of individuals in recovery from an eating disorder provides inspiration and validation. Others may wind up feeling behind and require reminders that the course of recovery from an eating disorder is rarely a straight line. It's also important to remember that some social media personalities may not be disclosing every aspect of their progress, including their setbacks, therefore, Facebook may function more like a Fakebook.

Alternatively, use of social media may keep some people stuck in a world defined by illness, rather than focusing on personal growth in other areas of life. When this is the case, people with eating disorders can be encouraged to develop a social media profile that is completely unrelated to food and body image, for example, by following people and outlets that align with career goals or other passions. Online and off (eating disorder or not), it's worth carefully considering how much time to spend looking at photos, new and old, of oneself and friends. If the amount of time spent scrolling through images is misaligned with a goal of body size acceptance, a change may be in order.

Focusing on: What makes things better or worse?

Eating disorders are complicated, and symptoms of an eating disorder may be improved, or worsened, by changes in a range of activities. For example, although more exercise would seem *always* to be a good idea, it may not be for a person with an eating disorder. It is important to identify when exercise turns into another symptom of a problem or leads to too much worrying about body shape. Individuals with eating disorders may become very upset about feeling unable to control some behaviors, like binge eating, without realizing that other behaviors that they view as positive, like skipping meals and never eating desserts, may also need to change in order to overcome the binge eating. It is extremely difficult to predict with confidence precisely what type and intensity of treatment will work for any given person. For some mildly ill individuals, self-help resources, a talk with a friend or family member, or a visit with their regular doctor may be all that's needed. For many, treatment with an experienced specialist will be required and effective. A generalist healthcare provider can also be of help, especially if access to specialists is limited. For a few, intensive treatments, like day programs or hospitals, will be necessary.

Two principles are crucial. First, the earlier the intervention is made, the more likely it is to be successful. Second, if the current treatment isn't producing results, change it.

6

DO EATING DISORDERS OVERLAP WITH OTHER PSYCHIATRIC DISORDERS?

Eating disorders do not occur in a vacuum. They have a high rate of overlap with depression and anxiety and a few other kinds of psychiatric disorders, which we will review in this chapter. The order in which an eating disorder develops in relation to another disorder can take one of three forms:

- Another psychiatric problem predates the start of the eating disorder.
- The disorders begin more or less simultaneously.
- Another disorder occurs later, following recovery from the eating disorder.

The sequence varies widely from one person to the next. Similarly, many individuals who develop an eating disorder never have another psychiatric diagnosis, and most of those with other psychiatric problems do not go on to develop an eating disorder. We must acknowledge, however, that the presence of multiple disorders simultaneously can complicate the identification of an eating disorder, as described in Chapter 3, and its treatment, as described in Chapters 11 and 12.

What other kinds of psychiatric problems do people with eating disorders have?

Depression

Depression—formally called *major depressive disorder*—is a type of mood disorder. People with depression experience symptoms including persistent low mood, loss of pleasure in activities previously considered enjoyable, low energy, poor concentration, disturbances in sleep, appetite, or both, and feelings or thoughts of worthlessness and hopelessness (which are sometimes accompanied by feeling suicidal). Depression is the mood disorder that most commonly co-occurs with anorexia nervosa, bulimia nervosa, and binge-eating disorder.

Over their lifetime, 50 to 70% in individuals who have had anorexia nervosa experience an episode of depression. Depression is easiest to diagnose if it predates the onset of the eating problem or persists following weight restoration or a period of sustained maintenance of a healthy body weight. This is because several symptoms of depression develop in anyone who is starving (and will therefore improve with adequate nutrition), including:

- Low mood
- Withdrawal from previously enjoyable activities and relationships
- Low energy
- Poor concentration
- Changes in sleep patterns
- Lack of appetite

Approximately one-third to two-thirds of individuals with bulimia nervosa will have an episode of depression over their lifetime. With estimates ranging from 50 to 70%, depression is also the most common co-occurring diagnosis in adults with bulimia nervosa who seek treatment. Among individuals with binge-eating disorder, the rates of depression are comparable to those in bulimia nervosa. In fact, depression may be the reason why someone with binge-eating disorder first comes in for treatment; the depression also may be more readily identified by a physician at a routine checkup than the eating disorder. However, if binge-eating disorder goes unrecognized, treatment may not be as successful as it should be.

For example, some antidepressant medications may contribute to small amounts of weight gain, and some may interfere with appetite and contribute to difficulty eating at normal levels. These side effects may be especially problematic for individuals with eating disorders, and treatment providers need to know about both problems when they coexist in order to prescribe the most helpful medications (and help their patients consider all of the options). Also, one antidepressant—bupropion—should never be prescribed to individuals with eating disorders, especially those who purge. Patients and their healthcare providers need to regularly check in about all symptoms when both eating and mood problems are present.

As ARFID is relatively new to the category of eating disorders, less is known about its overlap with depression. Initial studies suggest that the vast majority (upwards of 80%) of youth with ARFID do not have depression or any other mood disorder at the time they seek treatment for their eating problem.

Anxiety

The DSM-5 category of anxiety disorders includes social anxiety disorder (social phobia), generalized anxiety disorder, panic disorder, agoraphobia, specific phobia, separation anxiety disorder, and selective mutism (with the latter two diagnosed primarily in youth). The rate of lifetime co-occurrence between anxiety disorders and binge-eating disorder is estimated to be between 56 and 65%, with specific phobia and social phobia being the two most common. Social phobia is the anxiety disorder that most commonly co-occurs with anorexia nervosa. While more research on risk factors for eating disorders is needed for definitive answers, the presence of childhood anxiety disorders—and specifically social phobia or generalized anxiety disorder—appears to put people at additional risk for the development of eating disorders. Based on early reports, as many as one-quarter of youth seeking treatment of ARFID are also struggling with co-occurring generalized anxiety disorder.

Social phobia involves a persistent fear of social or performance situations in which a person may be scrutinized by others or meet new people. People commonly worry that they will act in a way that will be embarrassing, or that they will be visibly anxious. They tend to avoid social situations, especially when they are believe they are likely to be evaluated by others; they may feel intensely anxious (and sometimes panic) when in them. Though aware that the fears are unreasonable or disproportionate to the situation at hand, the avoidance, anxious anticipation, or distress in the situation continues and interferes with the person's usual routine.

Social functioning is commonly affected by eating problems and, as described in Chapter 3, this typically takes the form of avoiding meals with others, feeling self-conscious about body shape or weight, or isolating oneself socially because of strict rules around eating or compensatory behaviors. When social anxiety and related avoidance are attributed to the eating disorder, social phobia is not formally diagnosed; these symptoms are expected to improve with treatment of the eating disorder.

Obsessive-compulsive disorder (OCD)

OCD, previously thought of as an anxiety disorder and now in its own DSM-5 category, is a problem characterized by recurrent and unwanted thoughts, feelings, ideas, or sensations (i.e., obsessions) and by behaviors a person feels driven to do over and over again (i.e., compulsions). Typically, compulsions are carried out to get rid of obsessions.

Obsessions and compulsions related to food, body shape or weight, or exercise are not included for the diagnosis of OCD. These features, if present, are often better accounted for by an eating disorder diagnosis. The link between OCD and anorexia nervosa is especially compelling because of similarities between the two conditions (namely, obsessional thought patterns and stereotyped behaviors), though rates of OCD are elevated among people with bulimia nervosa as well.

In efforts to expand our understanding of the contribution of genes to the development of psychiatric symptoms and disorders, some evidence has been discovered that OCD and eating disorders, especially anorexia nervosa, may share some genetic influences. This could explain why a subgroup of people with anorexia nervosa also have OCD. (See Chapter 18 for more information about how genes contribute to these complex disorders.) When OCD is present in those with anorexia nervosa, it usually predates the start of the eating disorder.

Though data on ARFID are limited, a large study in adolescent medicine found that approximately 6% of youth with ARFID also meet criteria for OCD. Poor nutrition and the resulting state of starvation can worsen features of OCD (similar to how starvation can produce symptoms of depression, as described earlier). OCD symptoms experienced by an individual with anorexia nervosa or ARFID only while in a starved state can be expected to resolve with weight restoration.

Substance use disorders

Substance use disorders involve repeated, problematic use of alcohol, drugs, or both. Indicators of a problematic pattern include use that is risky (e.g., driving while under the influence), affecting day-to-day functioning (e.g., missing class, arriving late to work) or resulting in health problems or physical dependence.

One of the most intensely studied topics in eating disorders and co-occurring problems is the relationship between substance use disorders and bulimia nervosa. Approximately one-quarter of women with bulimia nervosa report problematic alcohol or drug use, or both, in their lifetime. One idea about why this might be is that individuals with bulimia nervosa and substance use disorders tend to share the personality trait of impulsivity. In fact, substance use disorders primarily occur in those with eating problems that involve binge-eating behaviors, also such as in binge-eating disorder and anorexia nervosa, binge-purge subtype (but less so in association with anorexia nervosa, restricting subtype). The relationship may be stronger in women than in men, though more research on sex differences is needed. Substance use disorders more often develop after bulimia nervosa, rather than beforehand.

As described in Chapter 2, some people with bulimia nervosa or anorexia nervosa, binge-purge subtype, purge by misusing substances such as diuretics or laxatives. This behavior is considered part of the eating disorder rather than a separate substance use disorder. However, the line is blurry when people with eating disorders are misusing prescription medications (such as the stimulant Adderall) or illicit drugs (like cocaine) to suppress appetite and control weight. A thorough eating disorders evaluation will include a variety of questions to determine the presence of a distinct substance use disorder, as explained in Chapter 3.

Trauma

Trauma—direct or indirect exposure to an event in which serious injury, violation, or death is threatened or experienced by an individual or a close friend or relative—is not, in and of itself, a psychiatric disorder. However, as mentioned in Chapter 2, experiencing a significant stressor, including a trauma, heightens one's risk for developing a range of psychiatric disorders, including an eating disorder. This appears to be the case whether or not the individual who experienced the trauma goes on to develop full-blown post-traumatic stress disorder (PTSD). Those who have eating disorders and describe a history of trauma will sometimes say that their symptoms—fasting, purging, binge eating—developed at least in part as (unhealthy) coping mechanisms for distress related to the traumatic experience. However, it is important to remember that trauma (much like childhood anxiety) is a *possible* risk factor associated with eating disorders and that it is shared with other psychiatric disorders as well.

How does a co-occurring psychiatric problem affect treatment?

The way in which the presence of another disorder impacts treatment of eating disorders really depends a lot on the sequence in which the problems developed, and on the individual. If the other psychiatric problem started before the eating disorder and has been successfully treated, then someone developing a treatment plan for the eating disorder may have a sense of what kind of therapeutic work will be required to go the distance and may be optimistic about the possibility of recovery.

When multiple disorders are present simultaneously, treatment may take longer and involve more twists and turns along the way. Fortunately, many of the medications used to treat eating disorders (reviewed in Chapter 11) are the same as those used to treat a range of anxiety and mood symptoms. Similarly, the evidence-based talk therapies (described in Chapter 12) for eating disorders overlap with talk therapies recommended for depression, anxiety disorders, and substance use disorders. Specific skills learned in a type of psychotherapy known as cognitive behavioral therapy (CBT) can be broadly applied. For example, in CBT for bulimia nervosa, a patient strives to normalize eating patterns and to develop and use alternate, pleasurable activities to delay a binge episode. In CBT for depression, a patient strives to schedule in a variety of pleasurable activities to complete regardless of energy level or mood. Moreover, the strategies taught to challenge problematic ideas can be just as readily applied to the belief, "I am disgusting," as to the belief, "I am a failure." In this case, while it may require more practice and, therefore, take more time and patience for patients to feel better and be less symptomatic, the treatment is robust enough that both problems can be tackled in tandem.

In other cases, it may make sense to address two co-occurring problems sequentially. An active, severe substance use disorder likely requires intervention before treatment of an eating disorder can begin. Conversely, the acute (i.e., underweight) state of anorexia nervosa must be addressed prior to treatment of a social phobia.

When another disorder develops following remission of an eating disorder, treatment of the new problem may be entirely unaffected or minimally affected by the individual's history of an eating disorder. Yet again, this depends on the person, the specific disorders, and the circumstances. The main concerns are as follows:

- Whether treatment of the current problem includes a medication that affects appetite, eating, or weight
- Whether symptoms of the new disorder affect eating- or weight-related behaviors (such as loss of appetite with depression, fear of eating with new work colleagues with social phobia)
- Whether the new problem rekindles any eating disorder symptoms, such as binge eating to cope (ineffectively) with the distress associated with the new problem

Focusing on: Co-occurring mental disorders

Eating disorders overlap with depression and anxiety and a few other kinds of psychiatric disorders, including OCD and substance use disorders. Some symptoms of depression (such as low energy), anxiety (such as worry about food or social eating situations), and OCD (such as counting calories or checking the size of one's body repeatedly) may look like separate problems, but they are actually part of the eating disorder itself. When there are distinct disorders and they begin more or less simultaneously, identification and treatment are likely to be more complex.

7

ARE CHILDREN AFFECTED BY EATING DISORDERS?

Unfortunately, being young does not protect kids from developing eating disorders. Research in children suggests that half of young girls and a quarter of young boys report dieting in a given year, with nearly a third of girls and 15% of boys describing eating that is abnormal enough to need a medical evaluation. Purging is less common, but the fact that it occurs at all is obviously quite worrisome. The ratio of males to females among younger patients diagnosed with eating disorders is a bit higher (1 boy: 6 girls) compared to the ratio among adults (1 man: 10 women). Although binge-eating disorder, other eating disorders among boys, and milder or atypical cases appear to be on the rise, this probably reflects better awareness and identification by health professionals rather than a true increase in the number of kids with problems.

The most common disorders and the timing of their onset are as follows:

- Pediatric feeding disorders—infancy and toddlerhood
- ARFID—middle childhood
- Anorexia nervosa—early to mid-adolescence
- Bulimia nervosa—late adolescence to young adulthood
- Binge-eating disorder—late adolescence to young adulthood

Early identification of an eating problem is associated with a good treatment outcome. It is critical when learning about eating disorders in youth to remember that most children will not develop these problems, and most of those who do will fully recover.

What is pediatric feeding disorder?

Pediatric feeding disorder is a term that has, until recently, not been precisely defined, but has been used to describe a range of serious eating problems often affecting very young children. Many of these children are born with problems that get in the way of their ability to eat, and they do not successfully acquire the motor skills necessary to eat on their own early in life, such as swallowing without choking. Sometimes a pediatric feeding disorder develops when a baby is born prematurely, sometimes it happens when a baby is born with problems in the gastrointestinal (GI) tract, and sometimes it happens for reasons no one really can figure out.

Specialists in this area have become very skilled both at using methods to ensure that affected children get sufficient nutrition to allow them to grow normally and at devising ways to help the children eventually learn how to eat on their own.

There is at least some degree of overlap between pediatric feeding disorder and ARFID. Studies are underway to determine exactly where the boundary lies between the two and whether it would be useful to consider pediatric feeding disorders a subtype of ARFID. It will undoubtedly take some time to sort this out.

What is ARFID?

As described earlier (Chapter 1), ARFID was introduced into the eating disorders section in the fifth edition of the DSM. It is a broad category that includes a variety of clinical presentations. The primary feature of ARFID is highly restrictive eating, but it is distinct from picky eating, a commonplace, developmentally normal pattern of eating for many kids. The difference with ARFID is that food restriction is so intense that it leads to low weight (or a lack of weight gain or growth in children), medical problems, or social problems, for example:

- Being unable to eat with friends, on play dates, at birthday parties, or sleepovers
- Refusing to try new foods in the school cafeteria or at summer camp
- Having great difficulty eating out with family in restaurants

Unlike individuals with anorexia nervosa, those with ARFID avoid certain foods on the basis of sensory features, such as texture or color; because of fears related to the process of eating, such as choking; or because of complete lack of interest in the food. The food restrictions have nothing to do with worries about getting fat, body shape, or weight.

In younger children, who may be unable to clearly express their thoughts about their appearance, it can be difficult to distinguish between ARFID and anorexia nervosa. Both conditions are associated with a lot of anxiety and distress around mealtimes. Research on ARFID is just beginning. Scientists are very interested in better understanding the disorder and whether some youth with ARFID will eventually develop anorexia nervosa.

What is the treatment for ARFID?

Broadly speaking, the most promising treatments being used for ARFID are behavioral interventions that aim to help normalize eating and, if necessary, improve weight. Though evidence proving these interventions are effective is currently lacking, they evolved from psychotherapeutic approaches that are well tested in other eating disorders. Rigorous research on the helpfulness of these psychotherapies is underway.

One type of psychotherapy for ARFID is a specific form of CBT called *exposure therapy*. This approach is described in detail in Chapter 12. The purpose of exposure is to provide people with learning opportunities in and out of sessions, chances to confront and manage fears and/or disgust with the coaching of a therapist and then independently. For people with ARFID, this might include trying foods

- considered gross,
- with an unappealing texture or color,
- of a different brand from what is preferred, or
- in undesirable contexts (for example, eating peanut butter while spinning in a chair if afraid of vomiting).

Although exposure therapy can involve unusual experiments, the goal is to increase the flexibility of eating behavior in order to improve nutritional status, achieve a healthy weight, or improve social functioning. Exposures are personalized—with the creation early on of a hierarchy that serves as a treatment road map—and kids work with their therapist to take on increasingly challenging experiments that are manageable yet difficult. Because the sessions are expected to be hard, they are usually longer than typical talk therapy sessions.

Another psychotherapeutic approach to ARFID is family-based treatment (FBT), also described in detail in Chapter 12. In this type of psychotherapy, parents are on the frontline as change agents and are therefore empowered, with the help of a therapist, to set up meaningful plans to encourage improvements in eating behavior. For example, therapists assist parents in selecting a food their child ought to try (reminding parents that they know best what foods will be useful to incorporate), setting up a schedule for repeated trials of the new item, and creating a reward system for the child's successes in trying (not enjoying, just trying!) something different.

Since some children with ARFID are quite young, other treatment approaches include parent-only behavioral therapy and multi-family parent group psychotherapy, in which a group of parents learn about the main principles of behavioral interventions and then troubleshoot with one another how to implement these principles with their children. Troubleshooting may involve lively role play of what happened at home when a new food was introduced, with group members offering support and suggestions, or crowdsourcing ideas from other parents for reinforcements (i.e., rewards) that their kids find compelling (commonly, screen time is a big hit).

Finally, because ARFID may include serious food restriction or complete food refusal, medical status needs to be carefully considered. More structured interventions, or even hospitalization or nasogastric tube feeding, may be necessary to assist with nutritional rehabilitation.

What kinds of eating behavior can create problems for children?

There are several types of eating behaviors that, though common, are known to increase the future risk of problems with binge eating and weight for a subset of vulnerable children. For example, eating in the absence of hunger during childhood predicts binge eating during adolescence, particularly for girls.

Secretive eating—eating with the intent to hide what or how much is being eaten—is another behavior that can signal disordered eating or negative attitudes about food for children. Behaviors that can signal secretive eating include the following:

- Food wrappers in a child's room or backpack,
- Unexplained missing food
- Excess weight gain despite a child's seeming to eat very little

Secretive eating in children is associated with being overly worried about body shape or weight, increased likelihood of problems with restrictive eating and purging behaviors, and symptoms of depression.

For children, the experience of loss of control while eating, regardless of the amount of food eaten, may be related to binge episodes experienced by adults. Children cannot always easily access food but may nonetheless feel the drive to binge eat, and what constitutes an objectively large amount of food can vary widely depending on where youngsters are in their developmental trajectory. While more than a quarter of overweight children and adolescents experience loss-of-control eating episodes regularly, normal-weight children can also experience this type of eating problem. Loss of control while eating, binge eating, and overeating in children all predict a higher likelihood of binge-eating problems (such as binge-eating disorder or bulimia nervosa) in adolescence and adulthood. This appears to be especially true for girls.

Is early-onset anorexia nervosa any different from classic anorexia nervosa?

In general, as we mentioned in Chapter 2, eating disorders begin during adolescence or early adulthood. However, occasionally, an eating disorder can begin *before* adolescence. This has been well documented for anorexia nervosa: A small number of cases begin just at the start of puberty or even before, as young as 8 or 9 years old. Perhaps surprisingly, given how young the patients can be, the features of the illness are quite similar to those of more typical, adolescent cases.

Treatment for young children is also quite similar to adolescent treatment. The family is an integral part of the process. In young children, as in adolescents, underweight is estimated by comparing body mass index (BMI; defined further in Chapter 14) to age- and sex-matched norms. This is referred to as a *BMI centile* or the percent of median BMI for age and sex.

Weight restoration goals are determined on the basis of BMI centile and the child's own growth trajectory. Because children are expected to grow over time, weight is a bit of a moving target. It is important for parents to know that early identification of children with eating problems is associated with the best outcomes and that parents and pediatricians can work together successfully to help a child resume eating, gaining weight, and growing to predicted range.

Focusing on: Children

Children are not immune from feeding and eating problems. Pediatric feeding disorders, ARFID, and anorexia nervosa are the most frequently occurring eating disorders in youngsters. Though the onset of bulimia nervosa and binge-eating disorder tends to occur later in adolescence or in early adulthood, the hallmark feature of these illnesses—a sense of loss of control while eating—is experienced by some children. Early identification of an eating disorder and parental involvement in its treatment will help most children to achieve a full recovery.

8

IS OBESITY AN EATING DISORDER?

We are often asked this question. It has a simple answer: No.

To understand this answer, we need to start with the definition of obesity. *Obesity* is simply an excess of body fat; it is a physical state, not a behavior. Many influences contribute to whether someone becomes obese. These influences include the following:

- The genes a person was born with
- What kinds of foods a person is exposed to when growing up
- How much exercise the person gets
- What foods she or he eats

What people eat is strongly influenced by what food is available, and many experts worry that it has gotten a lot easier to become obese in the United States because there is a lot of tasty, high-calorie, and inexpensive food around, not to mention how much advertising there is for these foods (you don't see a lot of ads on TV for green, leafy vegetables).

Some eating disturbances, especially binge-eating disorder, may also contribute to obesity. But most people who are obese do *not* have an eating disorder.

As we mentioned in Chapter 1, a very rough analogy might be poverty. *Poverty* can be defined as not having sufficient money or resources to meet basic needs, like for food, clothing, and shelter. Many influences contribute to poverty, especially the economy, but a person's native abilities, their education, and what kind of support they receive from their family are also factors. In a few instances, mental disorders also contribute to poverty, but most people who are poor do *not* have a mental disorder. Similarly, most people who are obese do *not* have an eating disorder.

How is obesity measured?

A simple, commonly used way to determine whether someone is obese is to calculate their body mass index (BMI): BMI = (weight in kilograms)/(height in meters)^2. There are many websites on the Internet that will do this calculation, for example:

https://www.nhlbi.nih.gov/health/educational/lose_wt/BMI/bmicalc.htm

The usual guidelines for BMI in adults, both men and women, are summarized in Table 8.1.

For children and adolescents, the interpretation of BMI is more complicated because of body changes during growth and development. The following website is useful:

https://www.cdc.gov/healthyweight/bmi/calculator.html

Table 8.1. Weight categories in adults

Category	BMI Range
Normal weight	18.5–24.9
Overweight	25–29.9
Mildly obese	30–34.9
Moderately obese	35–39.9
Severely obese	40 or over

Of note, BMI does not specifically measure the amount of body fat. But, it turns out that the amount of body fat is closely related to BMI, so almost always, an adult with a BMI over 30 will be found to have excess body fat.

Is there any relationship between obesity and eating disorders?

While obesity is definitely *not* an eating disorder, it turns out that there is a link between obesity and eating disorders, especially between obesity and binge-eating disorder. Specifically, as the degree of obesity increases, the chances of someone having binge-eating disorder also increase. For example, a recent study found that about 3% of people who were severely obese had binge-eating disorder, compared with only 0.5% of people whose weights were in the normal or overweight range.

Does binge eating cause obesity?

Perhaps surprisingly, this is not entirely clear. It is certainly possible that binge eating contributes to the development of obesity in some individuals, but in others binge eating may be just another symptom of obesity or it may develop in response to dieting. We don't have enough information to be sure which of these alternatives is more likely.

There is a little more information about adolescents. Because normal calorie intake can be so high when kids are growing, it is hard to define what an unusually large amount of food would be. So, researchers in this area have instead focused on adolescents who describe loss-of-control eating episodes, when they do not feel able to stop eating once they have started. Some studies suggest that kids who frequently experience a loss of control while eating—that is, feel unable to stop eating at times—are more likely to gain excessive amounts of weight than are kids who do not describe such episodes.

Focusing on: Obesity

Obesity is defined as having an excessive amount of body fat and is not an eating disorder. The frequency of binge-eating disorder among very obese individuals is quite low, but it is higher than among individuals who are not obese. It is not clear whether binge eating contributes to the development of obesity or is better viewed as a symptom of being obese. However, there are indications that loss-of-control eating during adolescence may contribute to excessive weight gain over time.

PART II

TAKING ACTION

TREATMENT AND RECOVERY

9

WHERE DO PEOPLE
GET EATING DISORDER
TREATMENT?

Once an eating disorder has been diagnosed, decisions about treatment options may seem daunting. Quick Internet searches may lead to an alphabet soup of treatment offerings (CBT, FBT, IPT, DBT, etc.) and long lists of programs that may not include any of the familiar hospitals or healthcare facilities in the neighborhood or surrounding region.

Treatments for eating disorders generally aim to help people change eating behaviors and sometimes their weight. The main idea is to interrupt symptoms and resolve disturbing thoughts and feelings associated with eating and/or body shape and weight. These behavioral treatments may be provided in a number of settings, which differ in the amount of supervision available. The healthcare insurance industry uses the term *levels of care* to describe the different settings, with the highest level of care indicating the most intensive care setting (inpatient hospitalization), and the lowest indicating the least intensive setting (outpatient treatment, see Figure 9.1).

How is inpatient treatment different from residential treatment?

Inpatient and residential treatment are the two most intensive treatment settings used for the treatment of eating disorders. The reasons for using these settings include the following:

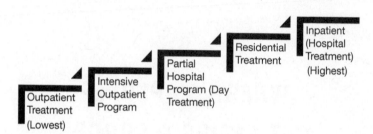

Figure 9.1. Levels of care in eating disorders treatment.

- Medical instability of the patient, including abnormal pulse, blood pressure, or lab tests and/or significantly low weight
- The need for support and supervision at mealtimes and throughout the day and night

While both inpatient and residential treatment include 24/7 oversight, meaning that patients live and sleep at the program and not at home, the two settings are different in a number of ways (see Table 9.1).

Inpatient programs for the treatment of eating disorders are situated on the medical or psychiatric units of hospitals. Medical hospital beds may be used for adolescents or adults who arrive with severe medical consequences of their eating disorders, and several medical hospitals have established protocols for the care of such individuals. Medical hospitals may initiate refeeding to medically stabilize patients and then refer them to a psychiatric hospital or residential setting. Hospitals devoted to psychiatric care may be the best hospital choice for the treatment of eating disorders when one is available, or when a patient's behavioral disturbances need relatively intense management. General medical hospitals may be the best choice when a patient has significant medical instability, or when there is no psychiatric hospital available and the patient is too unstable to be considered for residential treatment. Patients may progress from hospital treatment to

Table 9.1. Distinct characteristics of inpatient versus residential treatment facilities

	Inpatient Unit	Residential Program
Supervision	• Medical professionals available during all hours of the day and night • Frequent medical monitoring • Psychiatric units are generally locked	• Emphasis on daytime treatment • Limited medical monitoring • Medical professionals are not on site full-time
Interventions Available	• Medical and medication management; group-based therapies; individual and family therapy commonly offered • Option for nasogastric tube feedings or treatment over objection • Option for intravenous (IV) hydration	• Group, individual, and family psychotherapy offered • Medication treatments are commonly supported
Patient Features	• Voluntary or involuntary admissions • Vary in medical stability	• Residents are admitted voluntarily • Medically stable

residential or another level of care. Clinical teams recommend settings that are appropriate for the patient's level of medical severity and that are accessible, based on the patient's health insurance plan. Additionally, patient and family choice and a patient's prior treatment experience play a role in the selection of treatment setting.

What does a patient do during inpatient or residential treatment for eating disorders?

Inpatient and residential treatment programs for eating disorders generally include a set schedule of group therapy and therapeutic meals. Individual and family therapy are commonly included as well. Many therapy groups emphasize skill-building and behavioral change and may include principles of cognitive behavioral therapy (CBT). Other groups are supportive in nature and may include stress reduction strategies, working on relationships, and discharge planning and preparation. Patients tend to eat together, with staff supervision. They receive prescribed calorie levels and nutritional plans appropriate for their diagnosis and the severity of their disorder. After eating, there is typically a group discussion about the experience of eating, led by staff who joined the meal. This is followed by a period of supervision by the staff, designed to help patients manage any urges that would keep the eating disorder going and interfere with their recovery, such as self-induced vomiting or exercise.

Programs with a high level of care generally structure the eating plan around healthy eating and achieving a healthy weight. Many programs include a protocol for stepped increases in amounts and types of food. Nutritional plans that emphasize weight gain will commonly use nutritional supplements (e.g., Ensure, Boost, etc.) to help patients consume adequate numbers of calories during this phase of treatment. Programs may use an activity system to help reinforce progress. For example, patients may be restricted to the unit when first admitted, but may then earn staff-accompanied outings when they are medically stable and have met eating or weight improvement goals. Typically, as patients progress through structured programs, they are ready for and benefit from more independence, from choosing what to eat from a menu or baking with peers, to going clothes shopping with the support of clinical staff.

What is involuntary treatment?

Some patients are reluctant to seek treatment. Fears of weight change and of eating normally make many patients worry about what treatment may require them to do. For patients whose eating disorders are associated with severe medical or psychiatric complications, families or healthcare providers may want to encourage treatment even when a patient says he or she does not want to go.

Most treatments available for eating disorders are available only to patients who agree to participate—to be admitted to a program or attend an outpatient session. Psychiatric hospitals, however, have mechanisms to admit patients involuntarily if patients are considered to be an acute danger to themselves or others and if they are considered to have impaired capacity to make health-related decisions for themselves.

Each state in the United States, and every country, has different policies and procedures about patients' rights and about hospitalization and treatment over a patient's objection. In New York State, for example, involuntary hospitalization may take place if two physicians certify that a patient is at imminent risk and lacks the capacity for sound healthcare decision-making. Patients may appeal this decision and bring the case to a judge for further consideration. Residential treatment programs are not considered hospitals, thus patients cannot be involuntarily committed to residential treatment.

Since children and adolescents are admitted to hospitals only with permission by their parents, there are many young patients with eating disorders who will say they are being forced to receive treatment, yet whose legal status is considered to be voluntary, because they were voluntarily admitted by parents or other legal guardians.

Hospital programs generally have extensive experience in engaging patients of all ages in treatment, helping them to recognize the need for treatment and to feel more like partners in the process. Many patients who are reluctant about or even refuse treatment at the beginning get to a point of treatment acceptance as their treatment moves forward.

What is intensive outpatient treatment?

Intensive outpatient treatment, or *IOP,* is a catchall term referring to the particular level of care that includes several treatment visits per week, commonly involving a supervised meal and possibly some talk therapy groups at each visit. This is a level of care that is more intensive than seeing an individual outpatient provider, but less intensive than what is offered in many other structured treatment programs, and the patient does not live at the facility. Health insurance plans created language around the IOP level of care to describe this intermediate-intensity service. IOP is commonly used as a step-down or transitional program for patients who have completed a more intensive hospital-based program. Not all insurance plans include coverage for IOP care. Some insurance plans are willing to use coverage available for partial hospital or day treatment programs in a more flexible way in order to cover IOP instead of another service.

What is the difference between an IOP and a partial hospital program?

IOP and partial hospital programs (PHPs) differ in the number of hours of treatment they include, but both are generally programs that include group talk therapy and supervised eating. PHPs are also sometimes called *day treatment programs*. Many treatment programs use IOP to help individuals transition from the more intensive PHP level of care to something less structured, en route to discharge from a specialized program to outpatient treatment in the community. Also, insurance plans may cover PHP and not IOP or vice versa, so treatment programs may offer both to accommodate more individuals. Although both PHP and IOP are technically outpatient offerings (because patients sleep at their own homes each night), they are distinguished from the lowest level of care, outpatient treatment, which we describe next.

What are outpatient treatment options?

Outpatient treatment refers to care delivered to individuals who sleep at their own homes and travel to attend appointments. This is in contrast to treatments that are delivered in residential or hospital settings and last for at least a few hours of the day. Most people who receive outpatient treatment see at least one provider for individual sessions. Because eating disorders include medical, psychological, and nutritional features, many patients see more than one provider. For example, a patient may see a primary care physician (to monitor medical stability), a psychotherapist (for talk therapy), and a nutritionist (for nutritional counseling) for outpatient sessions. Ideally, when a patient receives outpatient care from multiple providers, the providers work together as a clinical team, and a team leader will be identified who coordinates communication among team members.

Different outpatient approaches are recommended for different eating disorder diagnoses (these approaches are reviewed in more detail in Chapter 12). For example, younger patients with anorexia nervosa may receive family-based treatment (FBT) with a provider trained in this approach. Commonly, FBT does not include additional clinicians (e.g., individual therapists, nutritionists) beyond a medical doctor as part of the outpatient treatment plan. This is because the treatment relies on parents to carry out much of the refeeding and support needed during the treatment period. Treatment teams may differ based on the particular clinicians selected. Some psychiatrists are comfortable offering both psychotherapy and medication management, while others may not be trained in eating disorder psychotherapies.

For patients who need more supervision and structure than that offered by a team of outpatient providers, or for patients who fail to make weight or eating behavior progress using individual providers, more intensive outpatient approaches—such as IOP or PHP, as just described—may be recommended.

What do people mean by evidence-based treatment?

Evidence-based treatment (EBT) indicates that there is scientific evidence, most commonly published in a scientific journal, to support a particular strategy or approach to treatment for a specific illness. For example, CBT for bulimia nervosa has been examined with successful results in multiple published studies and is therefore considered an EBT with strong evidence for its use (for more on the evidence supporting CBT, see Chapter 12). The term is used rather loosely by treatment programs that may advertise that they offer EBT when actually they are using a treatment in some way that hasn't been studied (e.g., a CBT group led by a therapist who has not been formally trained to conduct CBT for individuals with eating disorders may not represent an EBT). It is also important to note that while residential treatment programs and other intensive treatments are commonly used to help adolescents and adults with eating disorders manage their symptoms, the treatments offered in these settings have not been thoroughly studied.

Treatment programs are beginning to collect information about short-term clinical outcomes so that they can offer patients, families, and providers more reliable evidence about what to expect in these programs. As more of this information makes its way into academic publications, it will help assemble an evidence base regarding these treatments. Currently lacking, and extremely important as we continue to learn about effective treatments, is information about how treatments with higher levels of care, such as residential treatment, compare to evidence-based outpatient treatments, such as FBT for adolescents with anorexia nervosa and CBT for bulimia nervosa.

What's the difference between different treatment options?

A quick Internet search or call to an eating disorders hotline will lead to a long list of options that can be very confusing. There are many different program names and many treatments described. When considering the options, it can help to think about the *what, who,* and *where* of various treatment possibilities.

• **WHAT** type of treatment?

Depending on the eating disorder diagnosis and the symptoms that need attention, specific treatment approaches will be recommended. For example, CBT is useful for treating bulimia nervosa, FBT is useful for treating adolescents with anorexia nervosa, and interpersonal therapy (IPT) is known to be helpful for treating binge-eating disorder. (For more on these specific approaches, see Chapter 12). Across all settings where treatments are delivered, most of the approaches for eating disorders will focus on behavioral change, since behavioral disturbances having to do with eating and weight are the core symptoms of all eating disorders. Additional elements of treatment may include medical management or nutritional counseling, offered by specialty healthcare providers with expertise in these areas (e.g., a registered dietitian for nutritional counseling, etc.)

• **WHO** offers these treatments?

Because eating disorders are multifaceted illnesses, healthcare providers from a range of disciplines may participate in their treatment. Some professionals may be trained in multiple interventions. For example, a psychotherapist (e.g., a psychologist, social worker, or counselor) may have training in CBT and FBT. Some physicians may have expertise in nutritional management. Other clinicians may provide specific interventions. For example, a registered dietitian may offer nutritional counseling but may not have the training to offer other parts of the treatment. Patients (or parents of patients) should have a clear understanding of (1) their clinicians' training and area of expertise, (2) what each team member provides and how each team member's role is unique, and (3) how the team members communicate with each other about the patient's progress. For more on who provides treatment, see Chapter 10.

• **WHERE** are treatments delivered?

Treatments for eating disorders are offered in a range of intensities and settings. Generally, the severity of illness and history of prior treatment response will be considered in recommending the appropriate setting or level of care for treatment. The level of care or dosage of treatment for eating disorders has to do with the number of sessions per week (the frequency) and the degree of patient supervision provided in the particular setting. This is analogous to having an infection, like strep throat, and being prescribed an antibiotic to take a certain number of times per day for a set period of time. Patients are then left to choose whether to follow the plan as recommended, whether to get a generic or brand name drug, and which pharmacy to use. To some degree, these decisions are made on the basis of considerations of cost and convenience. In the case of an eating disorder, a referring clinician or treatment team will generally recommend the best setting for treatment. Ultimately, patients, their families, or both will choose a particular provider or hospital for treatment based on considerations of location, cost (including whether the program is covered by the patient's health insurance), and recommendations of the patient's clinical team. If the patient does not have a healthcare provider at the start of this process, he or she may get recommendations as part of an outpatient evaluation or medical workup. This is akin to meeting with a new primary care doctor, describing having frequent migraines, and receiving a referral to follow up with a neurologist for specialty care.

How well do these programs work?

Unfortunately, information about how people do after participating in particular programs is not collected systematically. But, there is increasing pressure on programs to begin to collect and provide this information in order to help patients and families make informed decisions about where to go for help, and when. We do know that higher levels of care are the settings where weight gain (for those who need this) and behavioral change occur most efficiently. This means that the support and supervision available in an inpatient or residential setting help individuals move their weight toward a recommended range more rapidly than less intense programs, and that treatment in these settings generally helps someone get to the next treatment phase (e.g., weight maintenance, relapse prevention, outpatient management) more quickly than a lower level of care, such as a PHP or IOP.

What if treatment is not working?

While there are many recommended treatments for people with eating disorders, not every recommended treatment works for every individual. If you or someone you care about has been in treatment for some time without change to the symptoms that brought you or them there, something different may be needed. It is useful to identify measurable treatment goals, agree to these with the provider, and outline a general timetable for meeting the goals. For example, if weight change or interruption in binge-eating episodes is part of the treatment, the patient and provider should decide how much progress is expected each week and should outline the parameters of this process. (e.g., How long should it take to begin to see progress? How many fewer binge-eating episodes would signify progress? What will happen if target weight-change or decrease in a specific eating disorder behavior does not occur as planned?)

If treatment does not meet the goals agreed on by the patient and their team, something should change. Sometimes, something can be added to the treatment, such as a medication, another team member (is there a dietitian already on the team?), or an increase in the frequency of sessions. Sometimes, the lack of progress indicates that the patient needs a higher level of care. This means that if outpatient treatment is not working, a more structured outpatient program that includes supervised meals or even a residential or inpatient program may be necessary.

Do all patients need all the levels of care?

The simple answer to this question is no: Most patients do not march through all levels of care as a matter of course in the treatment of their eating disorder. Some programs have developed a stepwise approach to treating eating disorders in order to keep some patients out of the highest levels of care, if possible, or to help patients become successful as outpatients after having needed the highest levels of care for some part of their treatment. There are no data to support there being only one way to do this, and scientists in the field are becoming more interested in the question of whether early identification and prompt referral to evidence-based outpatient treatment might make some of the high-level care treatments less necessary.

What does treatment cost?

Healthcare in the United States is costly. Health insurance coverage has improved for mental health conditions, including eating disorders, with passage of the Mental Health Parity and Addictions Equity Act of 2007 and additional legislation that has followed to clarify and strengthen mental health parity. Despite these improvements, different insurance plans cover different amounts of medical and behavioral healthcare, so it is important to check with one's insurance company before assuming that reimbursement is available for a specific program or a specific type of treatment.

Government-sponsored insurance plans (e.g., Medicare, Medicaid) do not pay for treatment provided in many freestanding treatment facilities, owing to an antiquated piece of legislation, called the Institutions for Mental Diseases (IMD) Exclusion Act, that prohibits use of federal funds for treatment of adult patients offered in a freestanding behavioral health facility with a capacity larger than 16 beds. This legislation has gotten in the way of Medicare and Medicaid being used for reimbursement at freestanding residential and inpatient programs for eating disorders.

While people do not commonly pay entirely out of pocket for treatment, it may be useful to know the range of costs that may be associated with eating disorder treatment. Healthcare providers charge different amounts for outpatient care in different parts of the United States. For example, psychiatrists will charge $100–$200 per session in many parts of the country, but upwards of $200 in the New York City area. Psychotherapists will charge $90–$150 in some parts of the United States, but above that range in large urban areas. Dietitians will charge $75–$125 in many regions. PHPs will cost $350–$750 per day depending on the program, and residential treatment will cost approximately twice that of a PHP, for example, $650–$1,500 per day. Inpatient or hospital-based treatment will cost upwards of $1,000 per day and may cost as much as $5,000 per day in some multi-specialty academic medical centers.

What if someone has no insurance to pay for treatment?

Just as with other illnesses, healthcare for eating disorders is expensive, and its costs are most commonly reimbursed by insurance plans. Behavioral health treatments are notoriously less available than they should be, and for this reason treatments may seem to be available only to the privileged. Several things will hopefully improve this situation. First, legislative efforts to ensure mental health parity, meaning ensuring that mental healthcare is as reimbursable as medical healthcare in any insurance plan, have already helped make behavioral health treatments more accessible. Second, public insurance, including federally funded Medicare and state-funded Medicaid plans, generally reimburses for treatments received at academic medical centers and community clinics. Third, and importantly, efforts to disseminate EBTs have contributed to self-help versions of some EBTs, including descriptions of CBT for binge eating and associated behaviors and FBT-based family handbooks to assist families of young persons with anorexia nervosa.

Focusing on: Treatment settings

Treatments for eating disorders generally include several interventions that aim to help people change eating behaviors and reduce associated symptoms. Care may be delivered by a team of clinicians and may take place across a range of settings, depending on the medical and psychiatric severity of the patient's disorder. Treatment for eating disorders is commonly offered in a specialized unit within a general healthcare institution, or in a specialized program where all services are for individuals with eating disorders. Typical treatment settings include clinician offices (for outpatient treatment), IOP and PHPs, residential treatment programs, and hospitals.

10

WHO PROVIDES EATING DISORDER TREATMENT?

Eating disorders are complex conditions, and adequate treatment commonly requires a team (multidisciplinary) approach. Navigating the landscape of treatment providers can be overwhelming, but it is worth taking the time to really understand who's who in eating disorder treatment and what role they each play in helping someone get well.

Who's who on an eating disorder treatment team?

Treatment for eating disorders can be provided by a range of professionals (it's not like taking out your appendix, a job that can be done only by a physician, specifically by a surgeon). Different professionals have distinct, but often overlapping, sets of skills. Here, we describe the professions most commonly involved in the treatment of an eating disorder.

Primary care physician

A primary care physician oversees a person's overall health, and may be a

- pediatrician,
- adolescent medicine specialist,
- internist, or
- obstetrician/gynecologist, for women.

Often, a primary care physician is the first point of contact for a patient or family when concerns about an eating disorder surface. The physician may serve as a kind of port of entry into the healthcare system.

Primary care physicians play a critical role in diagnosis. When someone shows up at a doctor's office with a concern about weight loss or weight gain, or about physical symptoms such as vomiting or cessation of menstrual periods, a crucial first task is to determine whether the problem is due to an eating disorder or to something else, like an infection or a problem with the stomach or gastrointestinal (GI) tract. Obviously, psychotherapy or an antidepressant is not the correct treatment for an infection, so it is important to establish the diagnosis before beginning treatment!

Assuming that an eating disorder is the correct diagnosis, the primary care physician evaluates potential physical problems that the eating disorder may have caused. Such problems are largely due to body weight being too low (as in anorexia nervosa) or too high (as is the case for many individuals with binge-eating disorder), or to the physical consequences of disordered eating-related behavior (such as self-induced vomiting). These problems can range from minor or nonexistent to life-threatening, and it is crucial that they be monitored and treated, as necessary, until recovery is achieved. The frequency of visits to the physician varies greatly depending on the nature and severity of the problems being monitored (for more information on types of physical problems and how they are typically monitored, see Chapter 3). If someone's weight is very low, the physician may want to see the patient every week to be sure it starts to increase. If someone is inducing vomiting frequently, the physician will likely order blood tests to determine whether the concentrations of substances like sodium, potassium, and chloride are where they should be and may prescribe supplements if they are not. The physician may suggest a measurement of bone density, as this is sometimes low in persons with anorexia nervosa.

Psychiatrist

Psychiatrists are also physicians, so like primary care physicians, they have "MD" (or "DO") after their name. They went to medical school and then completed specialized training (during a residency), during which they learned about the diagnosis and treatment of mental disorders. Like primary care physicians, they can prescribe medicines, and that is often a role they play in the treatment of eating disorders. More specifically, several eating disorders are known to respond to antidepressant medications, and it is usually a psychiatrist who prescribes them. This is not always the case, however; if a patient is on a stable dose of an uncomplicated medication regimen for their eating disorder, or if there are no psychiatrists available locally, then a primary care physician may take on the role of prescribing psychiatric medications. Psychiatrists play a variable role in monitoring patients' physical condition and in providing psychotherapy. That is, some psychiatrists become very knowledgeable about the physical problems associated with eating disorders and play a lead role in monitoring and treating them. Similarly, some psychiatrists develop extensive expertise in the types of psychotherapies used to treat eating disorders and may provide such therapy themselves.

Psychologist

Psychologists are professionals who have studied psychology after college, in graduate school, and earned a doctoral (PhD or PsyD) degree. The distinction between a PhD (doctor of philosophy in psychology) and PsyD (doctor of psychology) is subtle with regard to clinical expertise. Those with a PhD are considered experts of research in psychology, and those who specialize in clinical psychology (as opposed to other domains such as neuroscience or developmental psychology) receive extensive training in conducting original research related to mental disorders. Individuals with a PhD and those with a PsyD both receive extensive training in the delivery of different psychotherapies and different modalities (e.g., individual, couples, group) for a range of patient populations. Generally, psychologists are not able to prescribe medications for mental disorders. However, in a few states, it is possible for them do so after receiving additional training.

Typically, however, psychologists are involved in the treatment of eating disorders because they have developed expertise in the forms of psychotherapy that have been found to be useful.

Social worker

Social workers usually have attended graduate school after college and have earned a master's (MSW) or, sometimes, a doctoral (DSW) degree. To become licensed for clinical work, social workers pursue additional clinical training, including supervised clinical hours in any one or a combination of settings such as hospitals, case management services, residential treatment centers, and private practice.

Social workers typically have special expertise in dealing with families. In structured treatment settings, such as inpatient or residential programs, social workers are the clinical team members who most commonly meet with patients' families. In eating disorder treatment, these sessions typically focus on

- improving the families' understanding of eating disorders and their treatment,
- facilitating a conversation, with an emphasis on problem-solving, between the patient and family members about how eating disorder symptoms play out in the home or family environment, and
- developing a preliminary treatment plan for the period after discharge from the program.

In general, and especially for those working in specialized treatment settings, social workers may become quite skilled in using the psychotherapy techniques used to treat eating disorders.

Psychotherapist

The term *therapist* is a catch-all used for clinicians who provide talk therapy. This can include psychiatrists, psychologists, social workers and practitioners with a master's (MA or MS) degree in the field of psychology or counseling.

Dietitian/Nutritionist

A registered dietitian (RD) or registered dietitian nutritionist (RDN) has completed a bachelor's degree in food science and nutrition, plus 6 to 12 months of supervised training, and has passed a national examination. The qualifications required to call oneself a nutritionist are not as well regulated as they are for physicians, psychologists, and social workers, and in some places, there are no formal rules about the use of that title. (Any clinician should be able to answer questions about their relevant training and experience.)

Dietitians and nutritionists are frequently involved in the treatment of patients with eating disorders. They give specific advice about foods and help individuals make balanced food choices and avoid patterns that might interfere with recovery.

Treatment team

The treatment of an eating disorder typically involves a team of professionals. A common arrangement is for a patient to see a psychotherapist (often, a psychologist, social worker, or counselor) who provides talk therapy, but also to see a psychiatrist if medication is prescribed. A primary care physician is seen periodically to monitor the patient's medical status. A dietitian is often consulted as well to assist with improving food choice, portion size, and nutrition education.

There are multiple ways for a treatment team to be configured, depending on the skills of the healthcare providers involved and on who is available. Two elements are critical: first, the talents and experience of the team members, and second, their commitment to frequent and clear communication among themselves and with the patient. Ideally, a patient can get linked to a team that is experienced in the treatment of eating disorders and is accustomed to working together.

Regardless of the constellation of the treatment team, there is typically an agreement among members about the identified team leader. This individual may be selected for any number of reasons:

- Frequency of contact with the patient
- Duration of the healthcare provider's relationship with the patient
- Proximity to the patient (for example, a school clinician)
- Degree of expertise in and experience with eating disorder treatment

No matter who is identified as head of the team, this person is instrumental in coordinating care among team members so that there is regular communication and to ensure that this responsibility does not fall on the patient or the patient's family.

Treatment teams work in collaboration with the patient to establish treatment goals. Treatment works best when the team maintains a supportive but firm stance in decision-making in the service of the agreed-upon goals; this protects the patient from the burden of making difficult decisions while ill.

What's the difference between a psychiatrist and psychotherapist?

As stated earlier, a psychiatrist is a physician—someone who graduated from medical school and therefore has "MD" (or "DO") after their name, who then completed a four-year residency in psychiatry during which they took care of patients under the guidance and supervision of more senior psychiatrists. (Child psychiatrists spend an additional two years in training, focusing on evaluating and treating children and adolescents.) Because they are physicians, psychiatrists are able to write prescriptions for medication.

A psychotherapist is someone who provides psychotherapy (i.e., talk therapy). There is no "psychotherapy" degree. However, the standard programs for educating and certifying psychiatrists, psychologists, and social workers include substantial training in psychotherapy. On the other hand, in most states there is no formal licensing requirement for a psychotherapist to have received such training. In fact, anyone can hang out a shingle and declare that they are a psychotherapist. In contrast, psychiatrists, psychologists, and social workers must be licensed by the state in which they practice; licensing requires that they document the training they have completed.

Who provides psychotherapy for an eating disorder?

Talk therapy for an eating disorder can be provided by any professional with sufficient training and experience to have mastered the form of psychotherapy being provided. Usually, psychotherapy is provided by a licensed psychologist, psychiatrist, or social worker. As in many professions, a clinician's skill is determined both by their training and by how frequently they have provided the therapy. Experience counts!

Therefore, in judging someone's credentials, it is useful to know where they went to school, where they received their training after school (postgraduate training), and how much experience they have had (see Table 10.1).

Focusing on: Treatment providers

A variety of professionals can provide treatment for someone with an eating disorder, including psychologists, psychiatrists, social workers, counselors, and nutritionists or dieticians.

Table 10.1. Questions to ask to assess a clinician's experience in treating eating disorders

Sample Questions
• What kinds of eating problems do you treat?
• How long have you been in practice?
• How much of your practice focuses on people with eating disorders?
• Do you specialize in working with patients of a particular age, or with a particular type of eating disorder?
• What kind of specialized training have you had?
• Do you routinely work with other professionals? What types?
• How do you determine if the eating problem is responding to treatment, and if it doesn't, are you familiar with other treatment resources?

Often a small team provides care, coordinated by an identified team leader. The choice of a treatment provider depends on several factors, including who is available locally, but a common important factor is the experience of the professional in treating the disorder in question.

11

ARE THERE MEDICATIONS THAT ARE HELPFUL?

Medications are one tool in the eating disorders treatment toolbox. Several different types of medications can be useful, even dramatically so. Sometimes medications are prescribed for short periods of time—days or weeks—but more typically, people need to take them for weeks or months to get the greatest benefit.

What medications are used to treat eating disorders?

There is no one medication that is helpful in treating all eating disorders. Different medications are useful for different disorders. But, before getting into exactly which medications are used to treat which eating disorder, let's review the broad categories (classes) of medications that are used.

Antidepressants

Antidepressants are undoubtedly the most frequently used type of medication prescribed for people with eating disorders. This class of medication has a long history. The first antidepressant, iproniazid, is a close relative of a drug used to treat tuberculosis (TB). It was discovered in the 1950s when doctors noticed that some people with TB, when treated with this type of drug, became surprisingly happy. Iproniazid was discontinued in the early 1960s because of toxic effects on the liver, but it led the way for the development of the first class of antidepressants, the monoamine oxidase inhibitors (MAOIs).

In the late 1950s, good luck also played a major role in the development of the second class of antidepressants. Chlorpromazine (Thorazine) had been discovered in the early 1950s as useful for the treatment of schizophrenia, and in the course of trying to develop new medications for schizophrenia, scientists came up with a drug called imipramine (Tofranil). Imipramine turned out to be not at all helpful for schizophrenia, but it was impressively effective for the treatment of depression and was the first member of a class of drugs known as the tricyclic antidepressants (TCAs), because their chemical structure has three rings.

The MAOIs and TCAs are clearly useful medications for individuals with serious depression and also for individuals with certain types of anxiety (and for individuals with bulimia nervosa), but they are associated with significant side effects and can be fatal when taken in an overdose. Therefore, the introduction of fluoxetine (Prozac), in 1988, was a watershed. Fluoxetine has roughly similar effectiveness to that of the MAOIs and TCAs, but it is substantially safer and causes far fewer side effects. Fluoxetine was developed to target a specific chemical in the brain—serotonin. It is the founding member of a family of antidepressant medications that came to be known as the selective serotonin reuptake inhibitors (SSRIs).

Since the arrival of fluoxetine, many other SSRIs have been developed and marketed, and they are all very similar to one another (see Table 11.1). A small chemical variation led to the development of serotonin-norepinephrine reuptake inhibitors (SNRIs). Medications in this class, such as venlafaxine (Effexor), target not only serotonin but also norepinephrine (another chemical) in the brain, but are roughly similar to the SSRIs in effectiveness and side effects.

Table 11.1. Summary of medication class, examples (generic [common brand name]), and common usages in treating eating disorders

Medication Class	Examples	Usage/Concerns in Treating Eating Disorders
Antidepressants	Fluoxetine (SSRI) [Prozac] Sertraline (SSRI) [Zoloft] Venlafaxine (SNRI) [Effexor] Bupropion [Wellbutrin, Zyban]	Helpful in treating bulimia nervosa and binge-eating disorder FDA cautions about using bupropion for anorexia nervosa or bulimia nervosa because of possible risk of seizures
Antipsychotics	Olanzapine [Zyprexa]	May assist individuals with anorexia nervosa to gain weight
Anti-anxiety Medications	Diazepam [Valium] Alprazolam [Xanax] Lorazepam [Ativan] Clonazepam [Klonopin]	May relieve acute anxiety, for example, around meals. Effects last only a few hours. Some risk of addiction with prolonged use
Stimulants	Lisdexamfetamine [Vyvanse]	Helpful in treating binge-eating disorder May raise pulse and blood pressure
Anticonvulsants	Topiramate	Helpful in treating binge-eating disorder and possibly bulimia nervosa May produce a feeling of being slowed down mentally

SSRI = selective serotonin reuptake inhibitor; SNRI = serotonin-norepinephrine reuptake inhibitors.

Obviously, antidepressants are called antidepressants because they are useful in treating symptoms of depression. But we have learned that they are also quite effective in treating other mental disorders, including many forms of anxiety,

OCD, and, as discussed in more detail later in this chapter, several eating disorders.

Side effects of the SSRIs and SNRIs are generally minimal but vary considerably among individuals and are significantly bothersome for a few. The most common side effects are as follows:

- Drowsiness
- Problems with sleep
- Problems with sexual functioning

However, a few individuals, especially adolescents, experience an increase in suicidal thoughts or feelings when beginning treatment with SSRIs or SNRIs. This is obviously a potential development that needs to be monitored carefully, especially at the start of a new trial of medication.

Bupropion (Wellbutrin) is an antidepressant that does not belong to any of the major classes of antidepressants just described. It is an effective medication, but in an early study of its use for individuals with bulimia nervosa, several patients developed seizures. It was never figured out precisely why this happened, but there was suspicion that something about having an eating disorder made patients more vulnerable to having a seizure during treatment with bupropion. In addition, the type of bupropion available at the time was immediate release, meaning it entered the bloodstream rapidly, possibly leading to levels that were too high. Since then, delayed-release forms of bupropion have been developed and are on the market. Nonetheless, because of the occurrence of seizures among people with bulimia nervosa taking bupropion, the US Food and Drug Administration (FDA) strongly recommends *against* prescribing bupropion for those with histories of bulimia nervosa or anorexia nervosa.

Antipsychotic medications

Since the introduction of chlorpromazine (Thorazine) in the early 1950s, many medications have been developed that are useful in the treatment of psychotic conditions such as schizophrenia. Psychotic conditions are disorders in which individuals have problems with reality testing. People with psychotic disorders may, for example, develop delusions—beliefs that are simply not true—or hear or see things that others do not (i.e., hallucinations).

Antipsychotic medications help people by reducing or eliminating delusions and hallucinations and generally allowing affected individuals to think more clearly. In addition, most antipsychotic medications help with anxiety. Because of the effect of these medications in other groups of patients, and because these are medications that have been associated with a side effect of some weight gain, they are sometimes considered for patients with eating disorders, specifically for those with anorexia nervosa. They are usually considered only when other treatments are not adequate for helping a patient normalize weight and calm their anxiety and agitation. Most recently, a study examining the antipsychotic medication olanzapine in anorexia nervosa identified a modest amount of weight-gain benefit without other adverse effects (see Chapter 16 for more details about this research).

Anti-anxiety medications

A variety of medications has been developed to treat symptoms of anxiety. Some of the most well-known anti-anxiety medications are diazepam (Valium), alprazolam (Xanax), lorazepam (Ativan), and clonazepam (Klonopin). These medications and others that are closely related chemically are also useful in helping people get to sleep and stay asleep. Other than making people feel sleepy, they have relatively few side effects. However, they carry some risk of addiction. Therefore, it is generally recommended that they be taken for only brief periods of time.

Other medications

Among some of the other medications used in the treatment of eating disorders, probably the most prominent is the recent introduction of a stimulant medication, lisdexamfetamine (Vyvanse), for binge-eating disorder. Stimulant medications, all of which are chemically similar to amphetamine, are widely used to treat children and adults with attention-deficit/hyperactivity disorder (ADHD). One property of stimulants is a slight reduction in appetite, so it makes sense that this type of medication could help people with binge eating. Used appropriately, stimulants have relatively few side effects, but they do make some people more anxious and tend to increase heart rate and blood pressure slightly.

It is important to be aware that, although the appetite reduction produced by lisdexamfetamine is helpful for controlling binge eating, people with eating disorders may be tempted to use it as a means to lose weight. This kind of misuse can lead to problems, for example, for individuals with anorexia nervosa who need to gain, not lose, weight.

Another medication occasionally used to treat eating disorders is topiramate (Topamax). This medication is generally used for seizure disorders (like epilepsy), but it also has effects on appetite. Several studies suggest it may be useful for the treatment of binge-eating problems. Because it tends to suppress nerve activity, topiramate can cause sleepiness or slowness and fogginess in thinking, which can be troublesome for some patients.

How do the medications used to treat eating disorders work?

All of the medications used to treat eating disorders affect the brain's levels of neurotransmitters, the chemicals that nerve cells use to communicate with one another. Some medications, like the SSRIs, target specific neurotransmitters (such as serotonin), but because of the vast and complex connections among nerve cells in the brain, a change in the level of one neurotransmitter produces changes in others.

Precisely how changes in neurotransmitter levels lead to changes in how people feel and how they behave remains quite mysterious.

Do these medications lead to weight gain?

People with eating disorders often worry that medications will make them gain weight. With a few exceptions, this is not true. Most of the SSRI and SNRI antidepressants now used to treat eating disorders do not cause weight gain. Anti-anxiety medications are not associated with weight gain, and, as described earlier, stimulants may cause a small amount of weight loss. The medications that are associated with weight gain are the antipsychotics. As discussed later, and more extensively in Chapter 16, this has led to studies of whether they could help in the treatment of anorexia nervosa.

Do these medications damage the brain?

Sometimes people are concerned that medications used to treat mental disorders will lead to brain damage. Over the many decades they have been in use, no convincing evidence has emerged to support the idea that antidepressants, anti-anxiety medications, or stimulants cause brain damage (as long as they are taken as prescribed).

The story is a little different with the antipsychotics. It has become clear that some individuals, especially if they are treated with antipsychotic medications for long periods of time, may develop rhythmic muscle movements, especially of their face and tongue, and these can be permanent; this condition is called *tardive dyskinesia*. The chances of developing tardive dyskinesia on olanzapine, the antipsychotic medication that appears to be of some use in the treatment of anorexia nervosa, are very low, but it is important that the doctor who is prescribing the olanzapine check periodically for the emergence of such movements so that the medication can be stopped before the problem becomes permanent.

How long does it take medications for eating disorders to work, and how long do people stay on them?

If medications are going to be helpful, patients can usually see some improvement—perhaps not immediately, but within a few weeks of beginning them. To get maximum benefit and to minimize side effects, it is often necessary to adjust the dose a bit to determine the right dosage for an individual. This means it may take a month or three for maximum benefits to be achieved. When a medication is first started, doctors usually want the patient to check in frequently, possibly even every week, to adjust the dose and monitor for potential side effects. The prescribing doctor will usually see the patient at least every month for the first few months until the dose is stable. Then visits may become more infrequent (perhaps once every several months), but patients are expected to check in with any changes in symptoms and any other health-related problems to ensure that the medication doesn't need to be adjusted.

Typically, once medications start working, they keep working as long as people stay on them. Occasionally, the benefits seem to fade over time, necessitating tweaking the dose or even changing the medication.

Unfortunately, it is difficult to provide clear guidelines on how long to stay on a medication that has proven to be helpful in reducing symptoms of an eating disorder, and guidance varies with the type of medication and precisely what symptoms are being targeted. For antidepressants, our general rule of thumb is to continue them for 6 to 12 months, and then to consider tapering them, especially if the eating disorder is resolved. Medications that are being taken by individuals with anorexia nervosa to help increase weight can be taken as long as they are helping. People who take stimulants to help control binge eating may be able to taper and stop the stimulants after several months, once the binge eating is under good control. But any weight loss associated with stimulant use will likely disappear once the stimulant is stopped.

What medications are used to treat anorexia nervosa?

People with anorexia nervosa have a number of symptoms that, in theory, would seem readily targeted by medication. As reviewed in Chapter 6, significant anxiety and depression are common co-occurring disorders. It is very surprising, therefore, that antidepressant medications are essentially useless for this disorder, both when people are underweight and after weight has returned to normal. Why antidepressant medications are so ineffective in this case is a major mystery.

Throughout this book, we have described how anxiety provoking mealtimes can be for someone with anorexia nervosa. Anti-anxiety medications, like alprazolam, have sometimes been used, particularly before meals, to alleviate such anxiety. Unfortunately, in general, they don't appear to be dramatically helpful and are not widely used.

There has been long-standing interest in the use of antipsychotic medications for treating anorexia nervosa, based on a few ideas about how such medications might be helpful. One notion is that anorexia nervosa is a psychotic condition; that is, some experts have suggested that the distortion of body image characteristic of the disorder is so profound that it is best classified as a delusion. We don't view it that way, as people with anorexia nervosa don't believe that their weight is different from what it actually is; they don't think that the scale is wrong and that they weigh 200 pounds, even though the scale shows that they weigh 85 pounds. Rather, they agree that their weight of 85 pounds is low by some standards, but to them it seems perfectly fine. The problem is more one of judgment or interpretation than one with reality testing. In any case, there is no evidence that the use of antipsychotic medication significantly alters the distortion of body image in people with anorexia nervosa.

Another reason that clinicians have considered antipsychotic medications as possibly helpful in treating eating disorders is that they have the ability to relieve anxiety and compulsive thinking about body shape and weight. A third reason is that the increased appetite and weight gain often associated with this class of medications might actually be helpful for individuals with anorexia nervosa during weight restoration.

In the last decade or so, several research studies have been conducted in which individuals with anorexia nervosa have been randomly assigned to receive an antipsychotic medication or placebo (an inactive pill) and are followed for weeks or months. Sufficient evidence has now accumulated to document convincingly that the antipsychotic medication olanzapine (Zyprexa) provides a modest degree of assistance in helping people with anorexia nervosa gain weight. In the largest study, reviewed in detail in Chapter 16, people with anorexia nervosa taking olanzapine gained about a pound more per month compared to those taking placebo. On the other hand, olanzapine had little impact on the psychological symptoms of the eating disorder. Therefore, olanzapine may be of some assistance during the weight-gain process, but it is not, by itself, a definitive treatment for anorexia nervosa.

What medications are used to treat bulimia nervosa?

Even though anorexia nervosa and bulimia nervosa are closely related disorders, medications are far more useful in the treatment of bulimia nervosa than that of anorexia nervosa. Specifically, over a dozen studies have compared an antidepressant medication to placebo, and virtually all have found that patients taking the antidepressant were much more likely to reduce their binge eating and purging and to generally feel better. In the early 1990s, the pharmaceutical firm Eli Lilly and Company sponsored several trials that convincingly documented that the SSRI fluoxetine (Prozac) was useful in the treatment of bulimia nervosa. These data were sufficient to allow the FDA to officially approve the use of fluoxetine for this eating disorder; currently, fluoxetine remains the only medication with FDA approval for the treatment of bulimia nervosa.

In the trials conducted in the 1990s, it was discovered that the most effective dose of fluoxetine for bulimia nervosa was 60 mg per day, higher than the 20 mg per day dose usually used when treating depression or anxiety. It is important that patients taking fluoxetine for bulimia nervosa take this higher dose, to achieve maximum benefit.

What does it mean that a medication is FDA approved?

In the United States, the FDA is charged with evaluating whether prescription medications are safe and effective. Without such approval, drug companies cannot advertise to doctors or to the public that a medication should be used for a condition. The process of obtaining FDA approval is time consuming and very expensive, and it requires the drug company to sponsor several large-scale trials of a medication for people with a particular disorder and to submit detailed information regarding the benefits and side effects of the medication for review by the FDA. It is only after such a review that the FDA declares that the disorder is an indication for the use of the medication and allows the drug company to advertise that information.

However, doctors are free to prescribe any medication approved for sale by the FDA, even if the FDA has not granted approval for a specific medication for the patient's problem. For example, the SSRI sertraline (Zoloft) is approved by the FDA for the treatment of depression, but not for the treatment of bulimia nervosa. (Pfizer, the company that makes Zoloft, never conducted the relevant research to submit to the FDA, presumably because Pfizer thought the investment would not be worth the increased sales of Zoloft that would result.) Nonetheless, since SSRIs are very similar to one another, there is good reason to think that sertraline, like fluoxetine, would be helpful for the treatment of bulimia nervosa. Therefore, a doctor who for some reason prefers to use sertraline can prescribe it for a patient with the disorder. Such "off-label" prescribing is entirely legal and very common throughout American medicine.

What medications are used to treat binge-eating disorder?

The typical patient with binge-eating disorder hopes to achieve three goals during treatment:

- Stop binge eating completely or at least greatly reduce how often binges occur
- Feel better emotionally
- Lose some weight

Based on multiple randomized controlled trials of a number of medications, it is clear that antidepressant medications help to control binge eating and improve mood. But they usually don't have much of an effect on weight.

The stimulant medication lisdexamfetamine (Vyvanse), which is used to treat ADHD, appears to reduce binge eating, help people with binge-eating disorder feel better, and lose weight, and it has received FDA approval to treat this eating disorder. Lisdexamfetamine has relatively few troublesome side effects, but, like most stimulants, it causes mild increases in pulse and blood pressure, which may be problematic for people with heart disease.

Focusing on: Medications

Medications can definitely play a useful role in the treatment of eating disorders, but different medications are helpful for different disorders. Antidepressants are clearly of help in treating the binge-eating characteristic of bulimia nervosa and binge-eating disorder, but they are not useful in treating anorexia nervosa. Anti-anxiety medications might, in some cases, provide short-term relief from heightened anxiety, but alone they are not a sufficient treatment for an eating disorder. Emerging evidence suggests that the antipsychotic medication olanzapine may assist with weight gain for individuals with anorexia nervosa, and the stimulant lisdexamfetamine is helpful in the treatment of binge-eating disorder. The benefits and side effects of medications vary across individuals and require periodic monitoring by a physician familiar with their use for eating disorders.

12

WHAT KINDS OF PSYCHOTHERAPY HELP EATING DISORDER SYMPTOMS THE MOST?

Although the landscape of helpful psychotherapies for eating disorders continues to evolve, several promising interventions are already available. They differ somewhat in theory and practice but share several features. First, these talk therapies focus on the present—on the here and now. They are more concerned with the current symptom cycle of the eating disorder, rather than with the exploration of ideas about how and why the eating problem developed in the first place. Second, these therapies are directive. In treatment, patients can expect their therapist to be actively involved—in listening, in teaching skills, and in strategizing with them about overcoming obstacles to make changes. Third, these therapies are structured. Therapists and patients work together to cover material that has been found to be generally useful for people in eating disorder treatment and to explore how this information ought to be personalized to make the biggest difference possible in thoughts, feelings, and actions. Perhaps of utmost importance, the aim of *all* of the kinds of psychotherapy that help eating disorder symptoms the most is to effect change in eating behaviors. If eating behavior changes (and for those who are underweight, if weight gradually normalizes), then the therapy is helping; if behavioral changes do not occur, this is reason enough to consider how the treatment plan ought to change.

What is cognitive behavioral therapy?

Cognitive behavioral therapy (CBT) is a psychotherapy pioneered by Aaron Beck in Philadelphia at the University of Pennsylvania in the 1970s. It has been tested for a range of mental disorders, including depression, anxiety disorders, substance use disorders, and eating disorders; the base of evidence supporting its use is extensive. Like antibiotics for infections, there is no question that it is helpful.

As it applies to eating disorders, CBT emphasizes the role of thinking traps and problematic behaviors in maintaining the particular disorder. For example, in the case of bulimia nervosa, food rules are thought to be driven by being overly focused on appearance as a way to feel good about oneself. These rules lead to restrictive eating, which makes people more likely to experience binge-eating episodes and to use behaviors like self-induced vomiting to "counteract" effects of eating. Instead, however, these behaviors keep the cycle going, disrupt normal fullness cues, reinforce guilt about eating and obsession with body shape or weight, and may lead to the development of subsequent, even more rigid, food rules.

CBT targets the cycle of disturbed eating behaviors, rather than how any one symptom or set of symptoms began. In CBT, patients learn about the risks of having so many food rules and of purging. They are guided to improve their overall eating pattern, and then to gradually reintroduce fear or challenge foods. Patients learn problem-solving skills for managing potentially triggering situations and practice critically evaluating and reappraising ideas that could keep the eating problem alive.

In CBT, the therapist and patient come together to dismantle the disorder systematically through a series of behavioral experiments and analysis of the data or, put more colloquially, evaluation of what actually happens when the patient tries something new. In a typical session, a patient can expect to:

- collaborate on a session agenda with the therapist,
- review homework from the last session (including food diaries, reading, and/or writing assignments),
- learn a new CBT skill or practice a previously introduced skill, and
- develop a plan for what to practice at home between sessions.

Sessions typically occur twice weekly for the first couple of weeks to help individuals disrupt the eating disorder cycle as quickly as possible, once weekly for several subsequent months to maintain new behaviors and practice more flexible ways of thinking, and then less frequently (every other week or monthly) to prevent relapse and ensure continued progress. Both the patient and therapist should have a sense of whether or not this treatment is an adequate intervention for the problem within 4 to 6 weeks of its start.

CBT is a first-line treatment for bulimia nervosa and binge-eating disorder. It can be delivered in individual or group format, though most studies have been of individual CBT. Several randomized controlled trials of CBT support its usefulness in helping people to reduce or entirely eliminate binge-eating and purging. On average, people receiving CBT are helped to reduce problematic behaviors not just more drastically but also faster than are those receiving other kinds of psychotherapy. Studies suggest that CBT is a superior stand-alone treatment to medication. In addition to improvements in binge-eating and purging behaviors, people receiving CBT also report improvements in mood, relationships, and how they feel about themselves overall. Notably, CBT targeting bulimia nervosa or binge-eating disorder is *not* intended to be weight loss treatment, and results from several studies underscore that no more than modest weight loss ought to be expected from the treatment.

Although approximately half of patients with bulimia nervosa or binge-eating disorder receiving CBT will experience full or significant symptom remission, unfortunately, not everyone gets better. The data for CBT for individuals with anorexia nervosa are both limited and mixed. Rigorous studies in the acute (i.e., underweight) stage of anorexia nervosa do not show CBT to be more effective than other forms of psychotherapy. These findings are a bit hard to interpret because the studies are small, involve briefer treatment than recommended by CBT experts, and have high dropout rates. There is, however, some indication that CBT may be useful in preventing relapse in people with anorexia nervosa after they have been renourished.

Thus, the two main current challenges for treatment researchers are (1) to make CBT effective for a wider range of people with eating disorders and (2) to find ways to make sure the changes are long-lasting. An enhanced version of CBT (CBT-E), proposed to be *transdiagnostic* (meaning that it focuses on commonalities among the eating disorders rather than differences), provides a more individualized intervention within the traditional CBT frame. CBT-E, for example, includes optional modules on problematic perfectionism and relationship and communication problems. Self-help delivery of CBT—either through books or smartphone applications as described in Chapter 13—is considered a valuable method for relapse prevention and for increasing accessibility of the treatment to individuals who need it.

What is exposure therapy and can it be used to treat eating disorders?

Exposure therapy—formally known as exposure therapy and response prevention (or, ERP)—is a specific form of CBT known to be effective in the treatment of obsessive-compulsive disorder (OCD), social anxiety disorder, and specific phobias. In ERP, patients work in and between sessions to confront what they fear without using ritualized, safety behaviors. The purpose of exposure therapy is to provide people a chance to see that what they fear is unlikely to happen and that even if it does, they will be able to manage it. In ERP for OCD, for example, a patient who is fearful of germs might purposefully touch a number of potentially contaminated surfaces without immediately washing their hands to see if they get sick (and to learn that they can handle it). Repeated practice typically helps individuals get accustomed to feeling anxious, sometimes to habituate to it, and always to act in the service of health and flexibility rather than to avoid scary stuff.

This approach distinguishes itself from the others described in this chapter because it is experiential in nature. In ERP for eating disorders, after creating a hierarchy of eating disorder–related fears—things like types of food, eating situations (for example, portioning at a buffet, ordering quickly off of a menu), and clothing (for example, tank tops, fitted pants, bathing suits)—the therapist and patient work together in every session to learn to tolerate fears without engaging in corresponding rituals (such as selecting low-fat foods, under-portioning, readjusting items of clothing). In a typical session, a patient can expect to

- face a previously decided-on fear with the coaching of the therapist,
- invite anxiety and rate the level of distress experienced,
- notice if and how distress changes over time,
- notice if the feared consequence occurs and its implications,
- collaborate with the therapist on how to keep practicing facing the same or a related fear, and
- develop a plan for the next session's exposure.

Exposure therapy sessions may be longer than typical talk therapy sessions. And, they may involve doing unusual things to trigger and maintain anxiety or other difficult feelings. For example, if a patient has a fear of choking on food, he may be asked to put a lot of dry crackers in his mouth and let them sit there, or to eat a few tablespoons of peanut butter without taking any sips of water. If a patient has a fear that eating salad with dressing on it will make her gain weight, she may be asked to eat it during the session while cinching a belt around her waist to mimic the feeling of fullness and fatness.

In the 1980s, when CBT was being adapted for bulimia nervosa, tests of exposure therapy did not seem to unequivocally add to the benefit of the treatment. However, toward the end of the twentieth century, as exposure therapy for the treatment of several anxiety disorders evolved as the treatment of choice, eating disorders researchers decided it was worth revisiting. Principles of exposure therapy are being applied in several ways for individuals with eating disorders:

- As a relapse prevention approach for weight-restored individuals with anorexia nervosa
- As a tool for reducing body image distress in weight-stable adults with bulimia nervosa, binge-eating disorder, and OSFED, as well as weight-restored and weight-stable adults with anorexia nervosa
- As a method of targeting overeating and binge eating in overweight binge eaters
- As a primary treatment for ARFID

Research on exposure therapy for eating disorders is in its early stages. To date, the one, small randomized trial of exposure therapy as a relapse prevention approach for adults hospitalized for anorexia nervosa showed that a relatively brief course of exposure therapy (12 sessions over one month) was associated with very slightly improved food intake, with the most improvement evident in patients reporting the most anxiety. In the single randomized trial of mirror exposure to reduce body image distress in adults with eating disorders who were maintaining a healthy weight, the intervention was associated with improvements in body-checking, body image dissatisfaction, and other eating disorder symptoms. There has also been a single proof-of-concept study of exposures to highly craved foods in overweight and obese binge eaters in which participants were asked to look at, hold, and smell food, take two small bites, and then put it aside. Finally, with the introduction of ARFID in the DSM in 2013, clinical researchers began developing and testing exposure-based interventions to help these individuals, who may have difficulty eating adequately owing to concerns about food texture or type, normalize their eating behavior as a mechanism to improve nutritional status. Given the usefulness of CBT for eating disorders and the helpfulness of ERP for anxiety disorders, this is an exciting area of ongoing study.

What is family-based treatment?

Family-based treatment (FBT) is a psychotherapy that has been well studied in adolescents with anorexia nervosa. FBT is sometimes referred to as the *Maudsley Method* because of its origins at the Maudsley Hospital in England in the 1980s. Generally, FBT puts the patient's parents at the forefront of the battle with the eating disorder and encourages other members of the household—siblings, caretakers, and others—to provide practical and emotional support.

The theory underlying FBT is that, because eating disorders interfere with normal adolescent development, parental involvement is as essential in treatment as it would be for a child with any kind of serious illness. The treatment evolves over the course of three phases. Phase I emphasizes the renourishment of the patient. Initially, parents take control of areas of the adolescent's life that may be affected by the illness, specifically eating and exercise. All meals are prepared and supervised by parents. In Phase II, parents gradually hand back control to their adolescent. What this means depends critically on the child and the family's circumstances, and parents are helped to determine the age-appropriate and child-specific correct degree of control and autonomy for their child. During this phase of FBT, an adolescent might resume eating lunch unsupervised at school, making their own after-school snack, or going to dinner with friends one to two nights per week. In the final phase of treatment, the emphasis is on returning to a healthy, balanced life, which, for a family with an adolescent, includes the typical developmental struggles that may have been ignored because of the eating disorder. When a family is fighting about curfew instead of calories, it's a good sign that the eating disorder is in check!

In FBT, as much as is practically possible, the family meets together with the therapist. Appointments are weekly at the beginning, and sessions become less frequent as treatment progresses. Very early in treatment, one session is devoted to a family meal. Families bring a typical dinner to this appointment, and the therapist coaches parents, siblings, and whoever else attends on how best to (1) support the child in improving eating and (2) separate the patient from the disorder. In a typical session, the family can expect to

- receive feedback on the outcome of their refeeding efforts (including weight),
- review challenges that arose between sessions and how they were handled,
- identify goals for the week, including next steps in normalization of eating, and
- anticipate and plan for upcoming challenges, with the therapist's support.

There have been a handful of randomized controlled trials of FBT for adolescents with anorexia nervosa, and the results are encouraging. The intervention appears best suited to patients younger than 18, who live at home with their families, and who have families able and willing to set aside other issues in the service of treating the eating disorder. Studies comparing subtle variations in FBT suggest that firm and consistent parental involvement is likely a key ingredient of the treatment. Clinicians therefore carefully evaluate whether families can be adequately committed to this intervention in choosing it over other options. For those for whom FBT is a good fit, the benefits appear to hold up in the long term. In a study of FBT in adolescents with anorexia nervosa, for example, the majority of adolescents no longer met criteria for the disorder three years after treatment completion. As a result of such promising findings, FBT has been applied to adolescents with bulimia nervosa, atypical anorexia nervosa (an OSFED described in Chapter 1), and, more recently, ARFID, as well as to somewhat older age groups (e.g., young adults who are living at home).

What is interpersonal psychotherapy?

Interpersonal psychotherapy (IPT) was developed in the 1980s as a short-term treatment for adults with depression. It has since been applied more broadly, including adaptations for people with eating disorders and as a prevention intervention for youth at risk for depression and loss-of-control eating.

Within the realm of eating disorders, IPT is recognized as a viable alternative to CBT for adults with bulimia nervosa and binge-eating disorder. In contrast to CBT, IPT does not directly focus on eating behaviors or body shape and weight concerns. Rather, the theory underlying the treatment is that disturbances in eating behavior occur as a response to interpersonal stresses and negative mood. The emphasis in IPT is thus on identifying and addressing the relationship problems that maintain or worsen mood and eating disorder symptoms. IPT outlines four specific types of interpersonal problems:

- Grief (i.e., difficulty coming to terms with the loss of a loved one)
- Role disputes, which occur when people have different expectations about their relationship (e.g., adult siblings experiencing frequent conflicts about caretaking responsibilities of an elderly parent)
- Naturally occurring role transitions over the life span (e.g., a change in job, the transition from adolescence to adulthood or to parenthood)
- A lack of meaningful relationships, loneliness, or social isolation

Treatment goals typically evolve from one of these areas and serve to encourage functioning as well as possible in one's current roles as well as adjusting to changes in relationships and interpersonal situations. Eating disorder symptoms are linked back to their role in perpetuating or maintaining interpersonal problems.

IPT can be offered as individual therapy or as group therapy. After an assessment during which a treatment goal is established for a specific interpersonal problem area, a typical session includes the following:

- Review of material from the week relevant to the assigned area
- Communication analysis, including of arguments or avoidance of communication around a conflict
- Exploration of alternative communication options, including the introduction of communication skills
- Role play
- Assignment of homework, typically related to communication

In group IPT, the group is thought of as a way to decrease social isolation, support the development of new relationships, and practice communication skills. In essence, it serves as an interpersonal laboratory. The group format also provides a unique environment for patients who may otherwise keep problems with eating behaviors hidden from others because of guilt or shame.

Controlled trials of IPT versus CBT for bulimia nervosa show that the time course of the response to treatment is clearly different between the approaches. IPT takes longer to achieve its effects than does CBT; because the reduction in bulimic symptoms tends to occur more quickly in CBT, IPT is considered a second-line psychotherapy for the disorder. However, it may be especially appropriate for people who have not benefited from a course of CBT, or for those who have a lot of trouble managing stressors in relationships at home, school, or work.

Rigorous scientific trials of IPT for binge-eating disorder, as compared to CBT or guided self-help versions of CBT, demonstrate that the treatment significantly reduces the frequency of binge eating. In contrast to IPT for bulimia nervosa, the amount of time it takes for IPT to achieve its effects is similar to that of CBT for binge-eating disorder. People with binge-eating disorder are known to commonly have other, co-occurring psychiatric disorders (e.g., major depressive disorder) and therefore have problems in several areas. It is possible that the focus in IPT on relationships and on communication is an especially good match for some individuals with this disorder.

What is dialectical behavior therapy?

Dialectical behavior therapy (DBT), originally developed to treat chronically suicidal individuals with borderline personality disorder, is a well-studied psychotherapy. DBT focuses on the regulation of emotions and the development of healthy coping strategies and interpersonal skills. Whereas a CBT approach tends to help people develop strategies to prevent a particular emotional response from being activated, DBT helps people to change the expression or experience of an emotion after it starts. This is accomplished by practicing skills related to mindfulness, acceptance, and metacognition (that is, thinking about one's thinking).

The basic premise of DBT for eating disorders is that disordered eating serves to regulate otherwise intolerable feelings in individuals who may lack sufficient strategies for managing emotions. Binge-eating and purging behaviors are thought to be a result of trying to escape or block unpleasant emotions that may be triggered by thoughts of food, body image, or other aspects of the self, and to provide relief from these feeling states. DBT treatment is traditionally staged, depending on the patient's needs, (1) to address suicidal or self-harm behaviors that put the person at high risk of death or self-injury, (2) to expose the person to emotional states they have been avoiding, like anxiety, irritability, sadness, or anger, (3) to discontinue or decrease binge eating, mindless eating, cravings, urges, and obsession with food, and (4) to enhance quality of life in areas such as relationships, careers, and hobbies. For those who do not experience suicidal thoughts or impulses to self-harm, DBT for eating disorders has been adapted to first target other, potentially life-threatening behavior, such as severe food restriction, and can be further personalized to suit the individual, based on DBT principles.

Traditional DBT can be delivered in an individual format, with or without a complementary skills group (discussed later). In a typical individual session, a participant in DBT can expect to

- review a homework diary card, which includes ratings of urges to binge, binge-eating episodes, mindless eating, food cravings, and food obsession;
- identify key links in a sequence of events that lead to a problematic eating behavior;
- discuss how to apply a DBT skill (including mindfulness, taking an opposite action, etc.); and
- discuss how to pair the skill with acceptance (for example, that the reality is what it is, that a situation causing pain

has a cause, and that life can be worth living even in the face of painful events or moments).

A skills group teaches traditional strategies for each of three DBT domains: mindfulness, emotion regulation, and distress tolerance. In eating disorder treatment, sometimes a fourth domain, "eatingness," is also covered. This module includes discussions about the ways in which our current cultural and nutritional environment can be invalidating of true physical and emotional health, as well as psychoeducation about weight regulation and the effects of starvation.

DBT groups have also become a standard offering as part of higher level-of-care programs (e.g., IOP, PHPs, residential and inpatient programs, as described in Chapter 9). In these settings, the group leader teaches specific DBT concepts, such as mindfulness or distress tolerance, and participants have a chance to practice the skills during and between group meetings.

DBT is considered a third-wave behavior therapy, evolving from CBT, which in turn grew out of an approach known as behavioral therapy. Of all the third-wave psychotherapies (which include acceptance and commitment therapy, compassion-focused therapy, and mindfulness-based interventions), DBT is the most widely studied in eating disorders, with most of the research being done on adults with bulimia nervosa or binge-eating disorder, rather than anorexia nervosa. In studies in which patients are randomly assigned to DBT (immediately) or be on a wait list (and receive DBT a little later on), being in DBT right away is clearly advantageous over waiting for treatment. In the few studies in which DBT has been compared to CBT, the first-line psychotherapy for eating disorders, outcomes at the end of the study were not significantly different. Because DBT has not been proven to be superior to CBT and is not as well studied for eating disorders as for other disorders, CBT remains the front-running treatment. However, DBT, a first-line treatment for people with chronic suicidality, self-harm behaviors, and difficulty managing shifts in emotional states, may be a good fit for those patients with eating disorders who also experience these symptoms.

How long does psychotherapy last?

Because psychotherapy is tailored to the individual seeking it out, it is challenging to offer one-size-fits-all estimates on how long it ought to last. In scientific investigations, a standard course of the psychotherapies described here—CBT, FBT, IPT, or DBT—is approximately 20 sessions delivered over four to six months. Increased length of treatment for anorexia nervosa, as compared to that for bulimia nervosa and binge-eating disorder, is typical, as more time is needed to address expected reluctance to gain weight and the pace of weight restoration is variable. In FBT, because sessions are spaced out as the family becomes more adept at helping the adolescent improve eating behaviors and weight, it is not unusual for treatment to last twelve months.

Outside of the research setting and in the case of anorexia nervosa treatment of adults (where there is, overall, less clarity about a winning psychotherapy approach), treatment commonly extends out to or beyond one year. Yet, this is not universally required. In fact, patients can expect to complete the majority of skill-building within six months of the start of CBT, IPT, or DBT, and for those with straightforward eating problems, this may be enough time for eating disorder symptoms to completely resolve. However, for those experiencing symptom improvement short of remission or who have co-occurring psychiatric problems (some of which are reviewed in Chapter 6), an extended duration of treatment within any of the types of psychotherapy described here may be useful. Additional months in psychotherapy typically offer the opportunity for the following:

- Additional practice of skills within the scope of the eating disorder
- Generalization of skills to other symptoms (such as anxiety or depression)

- Relapse prevention, particularly in the face of usual life stressors
- Continued progress in valued life directions

Some people who have benefited from a structured, present-focused psychotherapy choose to transition to an open-ended, insight-oriented talk therapy for ongoing support or exploration of themes related to their understanding of the development of the eating disorder. Others prefer to end treatment entirely and, if needed, to return to the treatment approach from which they benefited if they experience any bumps in the road in the future. The latter can be thought of as akin to seeing a physician for a booster shot of a treatment of known benefit, like a vaccine that helps one to stay immunized against an infection.

How long do psychotherapy benefits last?

Talk therapy is hard work, but the good news is that the benefits tend to remain with an individual well after the treatment has ended. In follow-up studies of CBT, FBT, and IPT, in which patients are asked about their symptoms between 8 weeks and 12 months following the end of an active treatment, improvements are, broadly speaking, maintained.

This makes intuitive sense, because the skills learned in the talk therapies described here can obviously be used in the future. For example, if an adolescent who participated in FBT loses weight unintentionally in the future (for example, because of a stomach flu), she can use what she learned about weight gain (or family members can use what they found helpful) to restore weight without a return to treatment. If a woman in recovery from bulimia nervosa finds herself experiencing urges to purge in response to eating unfamiliar foods while traveling abroad, she can use the alternative activities she and her therapist discovered were helpful in riding out this impulse during CBT (e.g., calling a friend, knitting, or planning a sightseeing itinerary for the following day). If a man successfully treated for binge-eating disorder with IPT has difficulty adjusting to a new job, he can rely on the communication skills he developed to approach conflicts with colleagues proactively and productively. In short, the treatments described here equip the patient with a set of skills that can be used in the future to handle re-emergence of eating disorder symptoms as well as other sorts of problems that may develop.

Which is best: Medication, psychotherapy, or both?

As described in Chapter 11 (and to be elaborated on in Chapter 16), olanzapine, the sole medication that appears to be helpful for individuals with anorexia nervosa, provides only a modest benefit in aiding weight gain. In the treatment of the acute stages of the disorder, food is really the most important medicine. The challenges of weight gain for a person with anorexia nervosa are numerous, including the need for consistent intake of a very high–calorie diet, the fear of fat or of becoming fat, and the expected fluctuations in motivation for change. Given these challenges, psychotherapy (or some type of professional support) is typically essential in the treatment of this eating disorder. The same is true for the other feeding and eating disorders characterized by highly restrictive intake, including ARFID and atypical anorexia nervosa (described in Chapter 1).

In bulimia nervosa, an eating disorder for which medications have been proven useful (see Chapter 11), studies indicate that (1) the use of fluoxetine (Prozac) alongside CBT adds modestly to the helpfulness of the psychological treatment, and (2) medication adds significant benefit for those patients who are not early or lasting responders to psychotherapies such as CBT and IPT. Research about the relative merits of psychotherapy, medication, or combined treatment for binge-eating disorder reveals a slightly different pattern. First, CBT is a clear winner as a stand-alone treatment relative to medication only. Second, medication plus CBT is superior to medication alone. And third, certain medications, when combined with CBT, improve weight loss outcomes for those patients with binge-eating disorder who are overweight and need to lose weight.

Taken together, the science shows us that psychotherapy has a very important role to play in the treatment of eating disorders. However, there are circumstances when medication may be recommended as a stand-alone treatment:

- When an individual does not have access to clinicians trained in evidence-based psychotherapies for eating disorders
- When someone is unable to meaningfully engage in talk therapy (for example, owing to fluctuations in motivation, lack of financial resources, or lifestyle factors such as work, travel, or child care obligations)
- When the patient has other significant psychiatric problems requiring co-occurring treatment

Focusing on: Psychotherapy

To date, CBT, IPT, and FBT are the clear standouts in evidence-based psychological treatment for eating disorders. CBT is the psychotherapy of choice for adults with bulimia nervosa and binge-eating disorder, with IPT a second-line option with a reasonable amount of data supporting its use. FBT is by and large quite effective for teens with anorexia nervosa and has been adapted for wider use. We do not have great options for adults with anorexia nervosa, but, in general, a behavioral approach that emphasizes improvements in eating behavior and weight is probably best. Third-wave behavior therapies such as DBT are being tested for patients with eating disorders, as are adaptations of ERP, a type of CBT of known efficacy for anxiety disorders.

13

ARE THERE OTHER USEFUL STRATEGIES?

In Chapters 11 and 12, we described treatments reasonably well reported on in the medical and psychological literature; these are usually considered the first-line approaches for treating eating disorders. The evidence that has emerged from research studies give us confidence in recommending treatments like CBT. In this chapter, we describe other interventions and strategies that many people find useful but, with the notable exception of guided self-help CBT, that have not been studied as rigorously.

What is nutritional counseling?

Because eating disorders are complex and can involve disturbances in psychological and physical health, a treatment approach that targets multiple areas simultaneously can be quite useful. Nutritional counseling for eating disorders is typically provided by registered dietitians with specialty training in this area. The dietitian's role and responsibilities vary depending on the treatment setting (e.g., psychiatric inpatient unit, residential program, intensive outpatient program; see Table 13.1 for examples). Sometimes, nutritional counseling includes practice with portion-sizing, grocery shopping, food preparation and cooking, or dining out in public (commonly referred to as *meal support*).

Table 13.1. Potential responsibilities of a registered dietitian during nutritional counseling

	Examples
Assessment	• Evaluate the patient's current eating patterns • Complete a thorough diet history, including eating habits prior to the onset of the eating disorder • Estimate an optimal healthy weight range • Monitor weight • Determine caloric requirements for weight change and weight maintenance
Education	• Clarify the metabolic changes that occur with weight loss and weight gain • Discuss exercise and energy balance • Discuss the role of carbohydrates, protein, and fat in the diet. • Address how to interpret food labels • Improve the patient's relationship to food through enhanced understanding of hunger, fullness, and satiety cues
Behavior Change	• Develop sample meal plans, incorporating caloric adjustments to meet weight gain goals, if appropriate • Guide goal-setting and provide support for the patient as he or she tries new "challenge" foods • Help the patient normalize eating patterns to reduce risks of binge eating, if applicable

Nutritional support in the treatment of eating disorders dovetails with the logic behind CBT, and it is expected that the clinician will, in the course of counseling, assist the patient in understanding the connections between thoughts, feelings, and behaviors and in developing effective coping and problem-solving strategies.

Nutritional counseling is commonly used in conjunction with talk therapy to support weight maintenance and normal eating patterns for individuals transitioning from care in structured treatment like an inpatient or residential program to an outpatient setting. It is also a useful addition to talk therapy when patients have a diet-related medical condition, such as diabetes, celiac disease, or food allergies, or co-occurring psychiatric disorders, which may need to be prioritized. Nutritional counseling can also help overweight individuals with binge-eating disorder with sequencing goals to reduce binge eating and to lose weight (if weight loss is recommended).

What kinds of self-help books can help?

Self-help books can fill a critical gap in awareness of diagnosis, treatment, and recovery. When access to specialized care is limited, motivation for treatment fluctuates, or bumps on the road to recovery occur, the best of the self-help books about eating disorders provide hope, reassurance, information, and strategies for the reader (see Table 13.2 for an overview of popular self-help resources).

Currently, the only rigorously tested self-help books are those that deliver treatment based on the standard outpatient version of CBT for bulimia nervosa or binge-eating disorder. *Overcoming Binge Eating: The Proven Program to Learn Why You Binge and How You Can Stop*, now in its second edition, is a widely available text of this sort. In what is known as guided self-help, use of a book like this is combined with a limited number of brief therapist visits to help patients implement the treatment strategies described. How guided self-help is delivered—in person or via the Internet, with a mental health professional or a primary care provider, and the number of sessions—varies from study to study. Overall, this approach outperforms comparison supportive interventions and helps patients achieve outcomes comparable to those with specialized treatments like CBT, IPT, and FBT (described in detail in Chapter 12). Pure self-help, in which a book is used in the absence of any clinician contact, is not as well studied, nor is the use of either form of self-help for the treatment of anorexia nervosa. In general, use of these books requires a very strong commitment to doing the reading *as well as* practicing CBT skills. E-mental health resources, such as the smartphone apps

Table 13.2. Popular self-help books

Cognitive Behavioral Therapy

Beating Your Eating Disorder: A Cognitive-Behavioral Self-Help Guide for Adult Sufferers and Their Carers—by Glenn Waller, Victoria Mountford, Rachel Lawson, Emma Gray, Helen Cordery, and Hendrik Hinrichsen

Overcoming Binge Eating: The Proven Program to Learn Why You Binge and How You Can Stop—by Christopher G. Fairburn

Feeling Good about the Way You Look: A Program for Overcoming Body Image Problems—by Sabine Wilhelm

---

Family-Based Treatment

Help Your Teenager Beat an Eating Disorder—by James Lock and Daniel Le Grange

When Your Teen Has an Eating Disorder: Practical Strategies to Help Your Teen Recover from Anorexia, Bulimia, and Binge Eating—by Lauren Muhlheim

---

Dialectical Behavioral Therapy

The Dialectical Behavior Therapy Skills Workbook for Bulimia: Using DBT to Break the Cycle and Regain Control of Your Life— by Ellen Astrachan-Fletcher and Michael Maslar

The DBT Solution for Emotional Eating: A Proven Program to Break the Cycle of Bingeing and Out-of-Control Eating—by Debra L. Safer, Sarah Adler, and Philip C. Masson

End Emotional Eating: Using Dialectical Behavior Therapy Skills to Cope with Difficult Emotions and Develop a Healthy Relationship to Food—by Jennifer L. Taitz

---

Education and Support

Almost Anorexic: Is My (or My Loved One's) Relationship with Food a Problem?—by Jennifer J. Thomas and Jenni Schaefer

If Your Adolescent Has an Eating Disorder: An Essential Resource for Parents (Adolescent Mental Health Initiative)—by B. Timothy Walsh and Deborah R. Glasofer

---

Memoir

Brave Girl Eating: A Family's Struggle with Anorexia—by Harriet Brown

Gaining: The Truth about Life after Eating Disorders—by Aimee Liu

Goodbye ED, Hello Me: Recover from Your Eating Disorder and Fall in Love with Life—by Jenni Schaefer

Table 13.2. Continued

Cognitive Behavioral Therapy

Life without ED: How One Woman Declared Independence from Her Eating Disorder and How You Can Too—by Jenni Schaefer

Restoring Our Bodies, Reclaiming Our Lives: Guidance and Reflections on Recovery from Eating Disorders—edited by Aimee Liu

---

See Resources section for complete citations.

described later in this section, may be especially helpful for people learning and using fundamental skills in the treatment of eating disorders (and, therefore, their symptom reduction as well).

Another important category of self-help books is what we like to think of as self-help to help others. These books educate families and friends about eating disorders and aim to help readers provide support to their loved one in ways that have been proven effective by scientific research (see Table 3.2 for examples). These books may

- offer advice for parents based on the fundamentals of FBT,
- give teachers, coaches, and school counselors an overview of eating disorders,
- provide guidance on how to intervene before the disorders become life-threatening, or
- help readers determine if the blurry line between disordered eating and eating disorder has been crossed and when to seek professional help.

Finally, there are a variety of memoirs (see Table 13.2) written by individuals who have overcome eating disorders. It is hard to predict who will benefit from reading which (or any) of these accounts, and certain memoirs may actually trigger symptoms or be otherwise problematic in the early phases of recovery. But, overall, the stories may help someone in the acute stage of an eating disorder (1) feel less alone or ashamed, (2) understand their symptoms as a product of the disorder, rather than their personality, (3) become empowered in the treatment process, and, eventually, (4) explore the range of experiences and narratives about what it means to be in recovery.

Can e-mental health resources, like smartphone apps, help?

Because technology is now ubiquitous, the application of e-mental health resources to eating disorder treatment and overall psychological well-being is of great interest to patients, families, clinicians, and researchers. In the past decade, there has been a dramatic increase in the use of a technique called *ecological momentary assessment* to study eating disorders. Ecological momentary assessment refers to the use of technology in behavioral research to assess individuals' experiences, actions, and moods as they occur in real time and in their natural environment. For example, some research now involves sending alerts to an individual's smartphone that ask them to complete a brief survey—perhaps about their mood, whereabouts, recent eating or exercise behavior—multiple times daily to track patterns in the moment and in a natural environment. Whereas ecological momentary assessment is not designed to be directly beneficial to the participant, *ecological momentary intervention*—the electronic delivery of interventions to people as they go about daily routines—is. An ecological momentary intervention for eating disorders might include, for example, reminding an individual of their goals before a particular meal (e.g., try a new food, eat slowly) and their underlying motivation (e.g., eat out at restaurants more comfortably, become more aware of fullness cues). By and large, scientifically based conclusions about the merits of these interventions are lagging behind technological advances. However, behavior change is hard, and keeping it up is harder! (Just ask anyone who has ever made a resolution to save more money, or go to bed earlier, or give up caffeine, etc.) Ecological momentary intervention, though in its early days, is a potentially powerful way to improve access to basic principles of eating disorder treatment, extend the benefits of psychotherapy beyond the therapy session, and support long-lasting recovery.

Currently, a number of different apps (i.e., smartphone applications) are available that may be useful for people with eating disorders (see Table 13.3). The landscape of apps is

Table 13.3. Popular smartphone apps

Eating Disorders Specific	Description
Recovery Record	This app includes self-monitoring (food records, thoughts, feelings, urges to use compensatory behaviors), personalized coping strategies, and a portal to connect with the user's clinician. It also contains components of CBT-based interventions for eating disorders. The app offers assistance with goal-setting in addition to the ability to set reminders. Additional features include meal planning, rewards, affirmations, and the potential to connect with others.
Rise Up + Recover	This app includes self-monitoring (food records, thoughts, feelings, urges to use compensatory behaviors) and encourages the use of coping skills during times of distress. Users can share motivational quotes, images, and affirmations and access additional eating disorder treatment resources such as podcasts, informational articles, and a treatment directory. The app can also export meal data to share with members of the user's treatment team.
Cognitive Behavioral Therapy	
CBT Thought Record Diary	Self-monitoring of thoughts is a common, cross-diagnosis CBT tool that serves as a basis for identifying and challenging problematic thoughts. This app helps users document their thoughts and associated negative emotions and then analyze and re-evaluate the beliefs.

(continued)

Table 13.3.   Continued

Eating Disorders Specific	Description
MoodTools	This app was developed to support people with depression and may be of use to individuals with co-occurring depression and eating disorders. It includes ways to monitor mood, thoughts, and behavior; analyze beliefs using CBT principles; and develop a suicide safety plan.
MindShift	This app is specifically targeted for adolescents and young adults with a range of anxiety problems. It includes lists of coping strategies for different types of anxiety, and users can mark the methods that work for them for easy future access. Information is conveyed using simple, clear language. Important concepts are displayed in a catchy way; both text and audio are embedded in the app.
Dialectical Behavioral Therapy	
DBT Diary Card + Skills Coach	This app includes self-monitoring (to track mood, urges, and application of DBT skills), DBT skill review, goal-setting, and an ability to graph data about emotions and/or behaviors across time in order to evaluate patterns.
General	
Breathe2Relax	This app is designed to guide users through a breathing technique called diaphragmatic, "belly" breathing. It can be programmed with inhalation and exhalation durations that match the user's own version of a deep, full breath. In addition, stress levels can be monitored.
Calm	This app offers meditation sessions. The length of sessions can be personalized, from 2 to 30 minutes, to suit the user's needs. Meditations can be guided, or set to "timer only" for the more experienced user. A variety of nature scenes and sounds are available to help enhance the relaxation process.

See Resources section for complete citations.

rapidly changing, and we fully anticipate that the examples provided here today will be updated as soon as tomorrow. We must caution that many eating- and weight-related apps on the market encourage restrictive eating and weight loss, and these are not healthy choices for patients with eating disorders whose goals may include (1) weight gain or weight maintenance, (2) flexibility with food choices, (3) cessation of calorie-counting or hypervigilance of macronutrient content, and (4) adhering to a regular schedule of meals and snacks.

The most common function of apps developed specifically with eating disorders in mind, such as Recovery Record, and Rise Up + Recover, is a simple focus on monitoring of eating behavior and meal planning. Rather than encouraging fine-grained attention to macronutrient content (i.e., how much fat, protein, or carbohydrate is in a food), monitoring on these apps allows individuals to fill in a text box loosely describing what and how much they ate or to take a photograph of their meal. These apps can be set to remind an individual to eat at regular intervals (or if a meal has been skipped) and can be personalized to query for the presence or absence of eating-disordered behaviors at or after mealtime such as:

- Self-induced vomiting
- Laxative use
- Restriction
- Binge eating
- Compensatory exercise

There is also an option for the user to provide information about how they are feeling (emotional state), hunger, and full-ness. Both apps allow for goal-setting around common behav-ioral targets in eating disorder treatment, such as regular but not excessive weighing, reducing body-checking, and util-izing adaptive coping skills if experiencing an urge to binge, purge, or restrict food. The apps make it easy to connect with treatment providers, by the patient either syncing data directly with their clinician or exporting and sending summaries of records to a clinician. When asked about their experience of Recovery Record, some patients said they found connecting to the clinician through the app to be supportive and treatment enhancing, while others viewed it as interfering and deterring.

Several other potentially beneficial apps offer elements of psychotherapies deemed especially helpful for the treatment of eating disorders. For example, CBT-based apps offer ways to monitor and challenge problematic thoughts; cope with anxiety, low mood, and stress; work through steps of problem-solving; and support (broad) behavior change. DBT-informed apps include reminders of distress tolerance and emotion regulation skills, which may be especially helpful to someone experiencing emotional difficulty *in that moment*. There are also several popular apps, designed for anyone to use, that offer guided meditation and breathing exercises with the goal of stress reduction and relaxation. All of these tools, in the palm of one's hand!

What's the word on wearables?

The first self-tracker, the weight scale, was invented over two hundred years ago. These days, the options for self-tracking skew more high-tech and include a number of wearables—smart electronic devices—which can be worn on the body as accessories; think Fitbit or Apple Watch. These trackers measure fitness regimens, daily steps taken, estimated calories burned, heart rate, sleep cycles, and more. The usefulness of this information depends highly on the psychological health of the individual obtaining it, and those with eating disorders can be quite susceptible to digital data overload. Studies suggest that regular health tracking is associated with the presence of eating disorder attitudes and behavior. Fitness tracking, in particular, stands out as a risk factor for eating disorder symptoms.

Experts are uncertain as to exactly why wearables may carry risk for a person vulnerable to an eating disorder. Perhaps the granularity of the information collected by wearables reinforces the vulnerable individual's tendency to overly focus on unhelpful morsels of data—be it macronutrient content or steps taken—and, as the proverb goes, the forest gets missed for the trees. Or, it may simply be that the tendency within an eating disorder to develop preoccupations about health and eating places one at risk for overuse of tools that provide measures of eating, fitness, or weight.

Focusing on: Additional treatment strategies

Although the treatment tools described in this chapter have been less rigorously researched than those outlined previously, they are nonetheless promising ways to help more people with eating disorders get the help they need. Nutritional counseling stands out as an especially helpful supplementary intervention to help people fully normalize their eating. Self-help books offer a way for those with limited access to specialized care learn the principles of evidence-based psychotherapies for eating disorders. They are also an invaluable resource for family, friends, teachers, and coaches, who may be supporting an individual with an eating disorder. Though there is no denying that technology has produced the latest evolution of self-help resources, such as smartphone apps, these should be selected carefully, with an eye on overall physical health and psychological flexibility.

14

WHAT DOES RECOVERY LOOK LIKE?

Full recovery encompasses physical, behavioral, and psychological normalization. Weight (and rate of growth for children and adolescents) is in an optimal range for the individual and is stable. Eating is normal and a variety of foods are consumed. Anxiety about shape or weight is minimal, if present at all, and small fluctuations in weight are tolerated without distress.

How important is weight?

Weight is one measure of health for everyone and thus is an important piece of data concerning the current physical state of an individual with an eating disorder. By no means is weight the only physical measure to track, but weight should be measured regularly, and, especially if it has changed substantially from a baseline healthy state, weight should be monitored closely.

Weight goals are best set in the context of the individual's weight history. For example, when children see their pediatrician for a checkup each year, their height and weight are plotted on a growth curve, and for an adolescent or young adult, these growth curves are often used to set a recommended weight range. Of course, recommended weight ranges for young people are a bit of a moving target because everyone is expected to gain weight and grow taller up until their early 20s. For adults, the recommended weight range may be based on a time when the individual's eating behavior and general health were in good shape and/or within the standard recommendations for adults. (In general, consensus recommendations suggest that a healthy BMI [weight in kilograms divided by height in meters squared] is between 18.5 and 25 kg/m². Useful guidance, as well as a BMI calculator, can be found on the National Institutes of Health website: https://www.nhlbi.nih.gov/health/educational/lose_wt/BMI/bmicalc.htm).

What is full versus partial recovery?

Full recovery from an eating disorder implies resolution or remission of the physiological, behavioral, and emotional features that defined the illness. In full recovery, the person previously affected by an eating disorder should either be back to their baseline status of eating, exercising, and thinking and feeling about their body that they had before the problem started, or be thinking, feeling, and behaving similarly to a sample of individuals who have never had an eating disorder. For example, a young person who is fully recovered from an eating disorder should be eating the French fries (and other foods) that she enjoyed before her illness took hold, and should display the spark, sense of humor, and other personality traits that were present previously. If an individual is worried about body shape and weight, the worry should not be more intense than what is common for a person without a disorder. Women without eating disorders sometimes worry about changes to body shape following a pregnancy, or may express some body dissatisfaction with postmenopausal weight change. Men and women alike sometimes feel a little uncomfortable parading around the beach in a bathing suit, but they do not avoid the experience; rather, they set the discomfort aside to enjoy the sun and surf. In recovery from an eating disorder, body concern and dissatisfaction would not be expected to be greater than these examples.

Because behavior change is difficult, and because people with eating disorders often have mixed feelings about the changes needed for recovery, it is not uncommon for patients to improve somewhat but not completely, sometimes insisting that modest change is all they really want. Changes that include some but not all of the return to normal functioning are labeled *partial recovery*. Examples of partial recovery include the following:

- A woman with anorexia nervosa or atypical anorexia nervosa who restores some weight but not the full amount needed to resume spontaneous menstruation
- An individual with binge-eating disorder or bulimia nervosa who decreases the frequency of binge-eating episodes but does not stop the behaviors entirely
- A person who consistently eats enough to achieve and then maintain a weight in the normal range, but without broadening the menu items beyond safe and generally low-calorie foods
- An individual who successfully interrupts binge-purge cycles but without normalizing an eating plan to include three meals per day

Many patients and families believe that partial recovery is all that is possible for someone affected by an eating disorder. This myth should be dispelled! Full recovery should be the goal of every treatment for an eating disorder and is indeed a real possibility for individuals affected by eating disorders. Full recovery is more commonly achieved, however, among individuals who have had an eating disorder for shorter periods of time, and chronically affected patients should feel proud of improvements, however modest, as many changes along the way to full recovery are difficult to achieve and sustain.

What type of eating pattern is associated with recovery?

Treatment for eating disorders generally emphasizes healthy eating. This means eating three meals each day and, for some, a few planned snacks. Eating disorders include eating disturbances such as

- skipping meals,
- restricting intake,
- binge eating, and
- grazing and nibbling throughout the day.

Individuals may think that their eating disorder can be treated by helping them change one part of the problem without having to normalize their whole eating plan for the day. For example, a patient may want his binge eating to stop, but continues skipping breakfast and eating a small lunch. Another may believe that grazing on small amounts of food throughout the day is not a problem as long as the total number of calories eaten adds up to an amount within a recommended range.

Actually, normal and structured eating is not only a goal for its own sake, it disrupts symptoms and protects a slip-up from turning into a full relapse. Because restrictive eating and meal-skipping typically set the stage for binge eating, the resolution of binge eating will be far more successful if an individual eats three meals a day routinely. And, if a binge occurs, hopping back on the three-meal-a-day train helps prevent restarting a cycle of restriction and binge eating.

Sometimes patients are reluctant to try eating according to this pattern. In bulimia nervosa, a condition in which many of the disordered behaviors originate as efforts to prevent weight gain, patients who are working on stopping binge eating and purging may believe they will gain a lot of weight if they eat three meals each day, even though there is no evidence that this occurs. Treatments for bulimia nervosa and other eating disorders should include psychoeducation regarding the benefits of stable meal plans and behavioral experiments to help dispel myths about the consequences of changing eating behaviors.

Why is variety the spice of a fuller life?

Does it matter what a person in eating disorder recovery eats as long as they are eating enough? Yes! As it turns out, there's evidence that eating a broad range of foods is associated with the best outcome and should be considered part of full recovery from an eating disorder.

Patients with eating disorders tend to maintain rigid eating routines. It is not uncommon for patients to report

- eating the exact same breakfast and lunch each and every day,
- adopting a limited list of preferred foods and selecting meals using this very limited list, insisting that they have judged other foods to be unhealthy, bad, unsafe, or not tasty to them, even if these foods were previously enjoyed, and
- having difficulty eating in situations that require flexibility, such as when traveling, eating family style, or ordering at a restaurant.

In treatment, people with eating disorders are encouraged and supported to reintroduce a full range of foods, especially foods that were previously eaten, and to set goals around enhancing flexibility along other eating-related dimensions (e.g., timing, setting). For example, several studies have found that, among individuals with anorexia nervosa who had recently gained weight and reached a normal weight in a structured treatment program, the number of different food items eaten over a several days' period was strongly associated with significantly better health one year later. Conversely, those who ate from a more limited list were far more likely to relapse during the year following program completion. Patients with bulimia nervosa or binge-eating disorder may believe they cannot be in the presence of certain foods if they are to avoid binge eating. Individuals with ARFID may feel unable to tolerate food with certain colors, textures, or smells. Successful treatment for these disorders also emphasizes expanding food variety and identifying the connection between better food variety, overall health, and life satisfaction.

What does it take to get used to the new normal in terms of body image?

With the exception of ARFID (see Chapter 1), body image distress is a common feature in eating disorders. Among the most challenging for patients are the thoughts about body shape and weight, and beliefs that one is too large or is unattractive in some way (either after changing weight as part of an eating disorder treatment or after maintaining weight in the face of strong desires to lose weight). Unfortunately, all eating disorder symptoms do not resolve at the same time.

Treatments commonly begin by emphasizing improved eating behaviors. Eating behavior and weight will likely respond to good treatment in a matter of weeks or months, but thoughts and feelings may take much longer to catch up with improvements in behavior. Understanding that this is the expected trajectory of change is sometimes in and of itself a help to someone with an eating disorder. Maintenance of a healthy weight (and abstinence from dieting) is critical to give the thoughts and feelings a chance to change. It is sometimes helpful to ask an individual with an eating disorder to consider giving the treatment-related changes a six-month or one-year try in order to see whether it's possible to accommodate the new normal and test out if it could feel acceptable. Almost always, the extended time allows for significant reduction in, or full remission of, upsetting eating disorder thoughts.

Meanwhile, when treatment has included weight change or when body image concerns are significant, therapy should include exercises that help the individual challenge his or her exaggerated beliefs. For example, if a person is certain that "everyone is staring at me because I'm so big," or "everyone is smaller than me," the treatment should include the patient's collection of evidence for and against these beliefs. At this stage of therapy, the ongoing work aims to chip away at the assumptions and automatic thoughts that the patient finds so upsetting. Additionally, if change to one's body size or shape has taken place, as is common in successful treatment for anorexia nervosa, treatment should include thinking about ways to help tolerate the change. For example, treatment goals might include getting rid of old clothes that no longer fit and purchasing new clothes that do.

How can someone in recovery deal with other people's attitudes and comments?

In today's culture, there's a load of attention out there directed at what we eat and how we look, and this can be especially challenging for someone who has or has had an eating disorder. Social media posts, discussion among friends and family members about their preferred diets, and comments about whether an acquaintance or a celebrity looks "hot" or "dope" or "thin" or "plump" can trigger thoughts about how one's shape or one's food choice compares to whatever or whomever is being discussed.

It is easy for a healthcare provider to tell a patient that watching and listening to others provides exposure to the world we live in, and that he or she will feel less upset over time. But, in reality, these are difficult experiences, especially for individuals who are new to recovery. Eating disorder specialists routinely help their patients consider how to limit the amount of time they spend on social media or how to curate their social media experience for optimal health (e.g., whom they follow, which medium they use). For real-world interactions happening in real time, sometimes it is helpful to remember that everyone's recommended diet and body shapes are different, and that an eating disorder can distort the way the comments and observations are experienced.

People also commonly work with their families and treatment providers to identify language that to them feels more comfortable and to appreciate the potentially positive intent underlying comments, even when the words used aren't just right. For example, some patients let their families know that they do not appreciate the family's usual conversations about diet and exercise when they come to visit, or they change their friend group to include more people who eat comfortably and fewer who maintain an unhealthy relationship with food. For some individuals working on recovery from an eating disorder, participation in support groups or advocacy organizations that work to advance healthy messages about body shape and eating becomes useful (see Resources for more information).

How can a support squad help with recovery from an eating disorder?

The process of achieving recovery from an eating disorder always takes longer and feels more difficult than initially anticipated. The process is near impossible without support along the way. Everyone's recovery story is different. Many rely on treatment providers, family members, friends, and other resources to achieve and then maintain the behavioral changes needed. Outcome is best when there is openness to using the available supports.

Most people will agree that, in general, long-standing patterns of behavior are hard to change. Neuroscience has taught us that many of our regularly practiced behaviors become habits and are executed by different parts of the brain than those responsible for learning things for the first time (see Chapter 17 for more information on research in this area). As a result, making changes to what we do requires significant effort. Behaviors adopted during the development of an eating disorder may be considered habits. In this case, making changes will initially require great attention, then prolonged practice and vigilance about not sliding back into old behaviors, especially during times of stress or times that may otherwise be associated with changes to one's eating, such as during travel, life transitions, or illness. Acknowledging the need for support is crucial to success.

But what *exactly* might recovery look like?

Case vignette

Maria is a 27-year-old graduate student who developed classic symptoms of anorexia nervosa 10 years ago, during her senior year of high school and first two years of college. As the illness began, Maria's BMI fell from her pre-illness high of 22 kg/m² to a low of 17 kg/m² during the second semester of her freshman year of college. Weight loss was accompanied by interruption of regular menstrual periods, highly regimented eating patterns, increasing time spent running on campus, social isolation from peers, and irritability with her parents.

She first saw outpatient providers during the summer following her freshman year, who helped her feel "better understood" but did not help her achieve much weight change. She returned to college for her sophomore year, but following expression of concerns by her roommates to her resident advisor, she was asked by school officials to take a medical leave only a few weeks into the semester. Maria spent much of the academic year in structured treatment, first at a residential treatment program, then in a PHP, and then saw a team of outpatient providers recommended by the treatment program she had attended.

Maria returned to college the following fall, where she lived in a single room and received treatment from community providers in her college town. She had reached a BMI of 22.5 at the end of her acute treatment, but was maintaining a BMI closer to 19.5 for much of the year. She believed this was sufficient, given the definition of normal weight. She ate carefully and monotonously, preparing her own foods in a dorm that allowed it. She rarely ate with friends, "afraid that it would be too hard."

At this point in Maria's disease course, she believed she was recovered from anorexia nervosa, but her treatment providers did not agree. They noted that her limited eating and socializing were not consistent with the baseline functioning she described before the illness began. They remained concerned about the lack of variety in her eating and the continued choice of running to fill her down time, especially on weekends. While her periods had returned, Maria described her cycles as "light," and her treatment providers were certain that this supported their view that she had achieved only partial remission of her illness.

That winter, Maria reported several episodes in which she returned to her room after working in the library and found herself snacking on foods that were stored in the dorm's communal pantry. The foods included cookies and crackers and, once she started eating one or two of these, she would eat rapidly until she emptied a sleeve of crackers or a box of cookies. She found these episodes very distressing and reported to her providers that this new eating pattern signified that she had "clearly recovered" from her anorexia nervosa. In fact, she editorialized to her therapist her belief that the therapist "must be happy now" that Maria had begun to eat larger quantities than previously.

Maria's providers did not view this development as recovery. While she was eating larger quantities of daily calories on some days, and eating some foods she had previously avoided, the new eating behaviors met criteria for binge eating, and this was by no means normal or recommended. Her treatment providers therefore added education about normal eating and normal weight, as well as strategies for eating sufficiently during meals and planned snack times in order to help Maria stop her binge-eating episodes.

During Maria's senior year of college, she began to notice that she was thinking less about food, weight, and body shape. She said yes to more social invitations and enjoyed these more than she expected. Without her noticing, Maria's weight increased a few pounds and her BMI was more routinely closer to 21.

Maria's providers were more optimistic at this point about her progress and hopeful that these changes would become more permanent. They were concerned, however, about Maria's plans to move to a new city following graduation, hoping that she would agree to remain in treatment, though recognizing that she would need to transition to new providers.

Maria maintained her weight but described that she was still prone to stress and noticed that stress made her "either eat less or eat more." She agreed to begin to work with a new therapist and scheduled her sessions before or after her work day. A year into "being a grown-up," as she called it, Maria felt confident that she could be far more flexible with eating and that she had met many new colleagues in her work in a research lab that "had no idea that I had ever had an eating disorder."

Now her providers, old and new, agreed that Maria had recovered from anorexia nervosa, with skills that would hopefully keep her well, even during stressful or difficult times to come.

Focusing on: Recovery

Recovery from eating disorders is a multifaceted process. It takes time and may require several phases of treatment in order to take hold. Individuals affected by eating disorders sometimes believe they have recovered sooner than their clinicians or families believe they have. Recovery is indeed possible and should include return to healthy eating, weight, relationships, and day-to-day functioning.

15

CAN EATING DISORDERS
BE PREVENTED?

Prevention is a holy grail in medicine: The perfect way to deal with any illness is to prevent it from occurring in the first place. This is equally true of eating disorders. All sensible professionals who specialize in studying and treating eating disorders would like nothing better than to be put out of business!

Unfortunately, this seems very unlikely, for reasons we describe next.

What are different types of prevention?

The field of prevention, and the terms used to describe it, were initially developed to deal with infectious diseases, which, historically, were among the greatest scourges faced by humankind. For example, in the eighteenth century, smallpox killed approximately 400,000 Europeans *each year*, including five reigning monarchs. In a landmark accomplishment, smallpox has been eradicated—wiped out—using a method called *universal* or *primary prevention*.

Universal or primary prevention is possible when virtually everyone in the population is at risk for getting an illness and when the cause of the illness is clear. Both are true for smallpox. Smallpox is caused by a virus, the variola virus, and it is very contagious. One of the signs of being infected is the development of a rash, similar to that which develops with chickenpox. Sores also appear in the throat and mouth, and when people cough or sneeze, viruses from the sores are spread and anyone nearby is exposed. The fluid in the skin rash also contains viruses that can rub off onto clothes and bedding. Most unvaccinated people who are exposed get sick, and one-third of them die. Therefore, the cause of smallpox is very straightforward—a virus—and everyone in the population who hasn't been vaccinated is at risk.

Universal prevention involves treating the entire population with something to stop the development of the illness—in the case of smallpox, a vaccine. Edward Jenner, an English physician in the late 1800s, discovered that vaccination with cowpox, a virus similar to smallpox but not very dangerous, made people immune to getting smallpox. The vaccine used to eliminate smallpox contained another, but very similar, virus. Beginning in the late 1950s, an international effort was started to eradicate smallpox by vaccinating everyone on earth. These efforts faced a range of challenges—technical, financial, and political—but were nonetheless declared a success in 1980. Smallpox has been eradicated from the planet, and therefore people no longer need to be vaccinated!

Two other approaches to prevention are worth mentioning:

- *Secondary prevention* aims to reduce risk among particularly vulnerable individuals and/or to intervene at the earliest moment after symptoms begin to emerge, before the illness has fully developed.
- *Tertiary prevention* focuses on individuals who have already developed an illness and is aimed at reducing the impact of the illness and helping people recover.

Is universal prevention of eating disorders possible?

Universal prevention of eating disorders is challenging. Unlike infectious diseases, which are usually caused by a single virus or bacteria, eating disorders appear to be caused by a combination of a wide range of things; these are called *risk factors* and include

- genes,
- environment,
- stage of development (e.g., adolescence),
- social stress, and
- emotional state.

This complexity means that universal prevention efforts must target many factors at the same time, because, presumably, some are more important for some individuals than for others.

Universal prevention of eating disorders is also challenging because most people, even when exposed to what we think are important risk factors, never develop an eating disorder. Therefore, for most people, preventive efforts are unnecessary.

In recent years, researchers have attempted to deal with these challenges by developing programs that target both eating disorder prevention and weight management using school-based educational programs. The programs provide guidance on healthy weight management, which is relevant for virtually everyone but also should help with the prevention of eating disorders. Such programs appear to be broadly useful, but it is unlikely they can dramatically reduce the frequency of the most serious eating disorders.

Is secondary prevention of eating disorders helpful?

The aim of secondary or targeted prevention efforts is to prevent eating disorders from developing in individuals at higher risk and in those who have begun to show symptoms. Two programs have been examined in some detail.

The Body Project is aimed at high school– and college-age women, especially those with increased concerns about their shape and weight, and focuses on helping them resist the social pressures to be thinner. Research has found that this program reduces body dissatisfaction, unhealthy dieting, and symptoms of eating disorders, especially binge eating. The Body Project involves group meetings and has been adopted by a number of sororities.

The Stanford Student Bodies project is an online program that addresses risk factors believed to contribute to the development of eating disorders. It seeks to help high school and college students develop balanced diets and improve their body image. In recent years, a related program, StayingFit, was developed to teach about healthy weight regulation more generally.

There is good evidence that these well-developed and rigorously evaluated programs are useful in improving attitudes about body shape and weight and in reducing eating disorder symptoms. It is less clear that they significantly reduce the development of full-blown eating disorders such as bulimia nervosa and anorexia nervosa, in part because the frequencies of these disorders are already, fortunately, quite low.

What about tertiary prevention?

With tertiary prevention the aim would be to reduce the longer-term impact of eating disorders once they have begun. From our perspective, this is best thought of as a part of the overall treatment approach, rather than as prevention.

Focusing on: Prevention

Prevention of an illness is the ideal way to deal with it, and in a few instances, like smallpox, prevention leading to illness elimination has been possible. However, because the causes of eating disorders are complex, it is difficult to imagine any program that could eliminate the occurrence of all eating disorders. Nonetheless, programs that target unhealthy attitudes about body shape and weight and unhealthy dieting practices appear to be beneficial for people at increased risk of developing an eating disorder.

PART III

EATING DISORDERS
RESEARCH

HOT TOPICS

16

OLANZAPINE

A NEW MEDICATION FOR
ANOREXIA NERVOSA

In this and in the following chapters, we describe three areas of active research:

Hot topic #1 (Chapter 16): a new medication treatment for anorexia nervosa

Hot topic #2 (Chapter 17): the application of modern neuroscience to probe eating disorders

Hot topic #3 (Chapter 18): the emerging understanding of how genes contribute to the risk of getting an eating disorder

The first two topics are based on work conducted by our group at Columbia University, and work on the last topic has been conducted by colleagues around the world. We hope that these descriptions of ongoing work will illustrate how cutting-edge research on eating disorders gets done and that they offer some hints about improved understanding and treatment of these disorders in the future.

What is olanzapine, this new medication?

As mentioned in Chapter 11, many psychiatric medications have been considered for use in treating anorexia nervosa, and several have been studied, including medications that have proven useful for treating bulimia nervosa. But none has helped in aiding weight gain or in reducing emotional distress in individuals with anorexia nervosa—until recently!

Over the last 15 years, a few small studies have indicated that olanzapine—an antipsychotic medication used to treat disorders like schizophrenia and bipolar disorder—might also help people with anorexia nervosa. Recently, our group at Columbia played a lead role in a much larger study comparing olanzapine to placebo (an inactive pill that looks just like the medication, sometimes referred to as a "sugar pill") and found that olanzapine helped patients gain weight more than placebo. We believe that the accumulated evidence demonstrates that olanzapine is the first medication associated with some benefit for individuals with anorexia nervosa.

How was this study set up, and what did it find?

This design of this study, called a *randomized controlled trial*, is the gold-standard method for evaluating whether a medication is effective. This type of research design is described in more detail later in this chapter, but briefly, here's how it worked in this study.

After agreeing to participate in the study, 152 older adolescents and adults with anorexia nervosa were randomly assigned to receive either olanzapine or placebo (the sugar pill) as part of their outpatient treatment. Neither the patients nor their doctor knew, until the end of the study, whether they were receiving the medication or the placebo. Study participants were treated at one of five academic medical centers (Columbia University, in New York, NY; Weill Cornell Medicine, in White Plains, NY; University of Pittsburgh, in Pittsburgh, PA; Johns Hopkins Medicine, in Baltimore, MD; and Centre for Addiction and Mental Health, in Toronto, CA). They met with a study psychiatrist every week for four months and received up to 10 mg of olanzapine or placebo pills.

It turned out that study participants assigned to take olanzapine experienced improvement in their weight faster (approximately 1.5 lb per month) compared with those assigned to placebo (who gained at a rate of approximately 0.5 lb per month). This modest weight gain in the olanzapine group was the average weight change among all participants assigned to receive the olanzapine, including some who stopped taking their pills before the study ended, and others who chose to take lower doses than the target dose of 10 mg daily. Analyzing all of the available information collected from participants is considered to best way to estimate the effect of the medication in real-world situations and with real-world patients, even though it may underestimate the impact of a specific medication dose. Unfortunately, compared with those taking placebo, study participants taking olanzapine did not report improvements in their mood, anxiety, or other psychological symptoms during the study period.

Why might a medication help in anorexia nervosa?

Both treatment providers and their patients have long been curious about medications that could help with the unrelenting drive to be thin that is central to anorexia nervosa. Patients will sometimes ask whether a medication might interrupt the endless thoughts of food, weight, and body shape that are typical of this disorder. Also, the depressed and anxious feelings that are common for people with this disorder often lead clinicians to wonder whether medications that help others with symptoms of depression and anxiety could be useful. Olanzapine and other similar antipsychotic medications have been considered because the notion that one is fat or may become fat held by someone who is significantly underweight seems similar to the beliefs of individuals with schizophrenia and other psychotic disorders that respond to antipsychotic medications.

Why was olanzapine chosen as something worth studying for anorexia nervosa?

Olanzapine was interesting to clinical researchers studying anorexia nervosa because it helps relieve psychiatric symptoms such as delusions (beliefs that are not based in reality) in other psychiatric disorders, and the beliefs of patients with anorexia nervosa have properties that are similar to those seen in delusions. Additionally, olanzapine is known to treat anxiety and agitation, which are frequent symptoms in individuals with anorexia nervosa. Lastly, olanzapine has been associated with weight gain. While this is often an unwanted side effect for people with other disorders, researchers were interested in whether this effect might benefit those with anorexia nervosa, for whom it can be quite difficult to gain weight (especially in outpatient treatment).

Olanzapine had been studied previously in several small studies; it is common that small pilot studies (test runs) precede larger studies that hope to answer more definitively whether an intervention is useful. It was by no means clear that the weight-gain side effect seen in other populations who take olanzapine would lead to weight gain in anorexia nervosa. Several other medications with known weight-gain side effects (such as older tricyclic antidepressants, described in Chapter 11) did not cause any systematic weight gain in studies of patients with anorexia nervosa.

What is a randomized controlled trial, and is this the type of study that was done using olanzapine?

A randomized controlled trial (also called by its acronym, RCT) is a study of one or more treatments in which the treatment of interest is compared to another treatment by randomly assigning participants to the study treatment or the alternative condition(s). In medication RCTs, the active medication may be compared to

- another medication,
- a placebo (sugar pill),
- a psychotherapy, or
- another treatment.

When a treatment is compared to placebo, it is called a *placebo-controlled* RCT. To assign the treatments in a random way, we used a computerized program to simulate a coin toss for each participant's assignment. This is considered the best way to answer the question of whether a medication is useful for a specific population. If participants are not told what type of treatment they are getting during the study period, they are considered "blind" to the assignment; similarly, if the study clinicians who interact with the participants are not informed about the treatment assignment, they are also considered blind to the assignment, so the study is called *double-blind*. This is a crucial feature of placebo-controlled RCTs because it prevents conscious or unconscious bias on the part of the patient or the clinician from influencing how patients respond. If patients (or the clinicians) know they are receiving the real drug, they will likely feel encouraged and optimistic and therefore do better, compared to patients who know they are getting an inactive placebo or sugar pill.

The olanzapine-versus-placebo comparison described in this section was a double-blind, placebo-controlled RCT in which both the study psychiatrist and the participant were kept in the dark about whether the participant was receiving olanzapine or placebo during the study period. Only the research pharmacist and the single staff member who had created the randomization list knew about the medication assignment.

Did the study find that olanzapine helped?

The study found that, when compared to taking placebo, taking olanzapine helped with modest weight gain in underweight outpatients with anorexia nervosa. Psychological symptoms, including obsessionality, anxiety, and other eating disorder thoughts and behaviors, did not change any more with olanzapine than with placebo. Several physical symptoms, including the ability to sleep at night, to concentrate, and to sit still, were rated as less problematic by participants who received olanzapine than by those who received placebo.

Why didn't psychological symptoms change with olanzapine?

We are unsure why the medication did not help participants with anxiety, obsessionality (preoccupations), or low mood. This is particularly curious to us because, as described in Chapter 6, weight improvement itself is known to improve psychological symptoms of anorexia nervosa, and olanzapine was associated with greater weight change.

One possibility is that the weight change was too small for participants to experience feeling better. Another is that the assessments used in the study were not sensitive enough to pick up the changes that patients might experience in a short-term outpatient treatment. Also, it is possible that this medication only affects weight and not other factors. Individuals receiving olanzapine should monitor their mood, anxiety, and other associated symptoms with their treatment providers as they remain on the medications. Also, olanzapine should be considered for use in anorexia nervosa as only one part of what is usually a multi-part treatment, including psychological, nutritional, and possibly medication aspects.

What's the right dose of olanzapine when it's prescribed for anorexia nervosa?

Our study aimed to use 10 mg of olanzapine per day for anorexia nervosa. This dose is in the middle of the range approved by the FDA for other disorders and was selected because it was used in some of the previous small studies.

Nevertheless, in recognition that individuals with anorexia nervosa may be more sensitive to the medication and that they often feel nervous about trying a new medication, the researchers started all participants on a low dose of olanzapine (2.5 mg) and increased it slowly. Also, any participant who reported significant side effects (most commonly fatigue) could request an even slower rate of increasing the dose. As a result, many of the participants did not take 10 mg, but rather took lower doses for the duration of the trial. On average, study participants reached 6–7 mg per day as their highest dose during the RCT.

Were there side effects from olanzapine?

The clinical research team was very careful about measuring effects and possible side effects throughout the study. Questions about these possibilities were asked every week, and blood samples were taken and other physical assessments were done intermittently to check for these.

We were glad to learn that the participants assigned to olanzapine did not have higher levels of side effects than those with the placebo. In fact, some physical symptoms, such as difficulties with falling asleep and staying asleep, with concentration, and with sitting still, were worse among those receiving placebo than those receiving olanzapine. In other populations, olanzapine is associated with potentially serious metabolic effects, such as increased levels of glucose (as one would find in diabetes) and of triglycerides and cholesterol. In this study, the frequency of these effects was very low and no different between the olanzapine and placebo groups.

Who should take olanzapine?

In the publication about this study, we described the benefits as modest and emphasized that this medication should not be used as the sole intervention for this complex disorder.

Olanzapine will likely be recommended for individuals who may need assistance above and beyond the behavioral interventions commonly used for anorexia nervosa (as described in Chapters 9 and 12). For example, it may be useful for people who are admitted to inpatient or residential treatment programs and do not gain sufficient weight, despite being presented with supervised meals and therapeutic activities. The medication will also likely be helpful for outpatients, like many of those in the study, who are not interested in more intensive approaches such as residential or day treatment programs. Anyone who is considering taking olanzapine should work closely with their medical team to be sure that there are no reasons—based on personal medical history—not to try this medication, such as the presence of diabetes, liver function problems, or high blood levels of triglycerides.

Is olanzapine a first-line treatment for anorexia nervosa?

Olanzapine is not a first-line treatment for anorexia nervosa. Behavioral treatments—in outpatient or inpatient settings—are commonly tried first. Children and adolescents with anorexia nervosa are generally referred for outpatient family-based therapy (FBT); adults may be referred for a behavioral therapy such as CBT. (These psychotherapies are described in detail in Chapter 12.) As explained in Chapter 9, if outpatient treatment does not help, higher levels of care are typically considered. Most treatment providers and programs recommend using olanzapine only if patients are not benefitting from the usually effective interventions.

Are there other medications like olanzapine that work for anorexia nervosa?

Olanzapine is one of a group of relatively recently developed medications that treat psychotic symptoms and mood symptoms in illnesses such as schizophrenia and bipolar disorder. Specifically, these are called the *atypical antipsychotic medications* or *second-generation antipsychotic medications* and are considered to have fewer side effects than the traditional first-generation antipsychotic medications (reviewed in Chapter 11) such as chlorpromazine (Thorazine) and haloperidol (Haldol). While several other medications from this group (e.g., risperidone, quetiapine, aripiprazole) have been studied in small samples of patients with anorexia nervosa, there is no solid evidence that these medications help with weight gain or other symptoms.

Should olanzapine be used in children and adolescents with anorexia nervosa?

Olanzapine and other second-generation antipsychotics have been studied for use in children and adolescents with schizophrenia and bipolar illness and have received FDA approval for use in these populations. There has been only one small study of olanzapine for anorexia nervosa in adolescents, and it did not suggest its use was beneficial; it also did not identify any problems with its use.

Currently, in practice, psychiatrists consider adding olanzapine to the treatment plan for adolescents with anorexia nervosa on a case-by-case basis.

Should olanzapine be taken indefinitely if someone has or had anorexia nervosa?

Our recently published study captured what happened for those taking olanzapine over a four-month period. Very little is known about the longer-term use of this medication for individuals with anorexia nervosa. Patients should only take olanzapine under the regular care of a physician (a psychiatrist, primary care clinician, or both). Regular monitoring of weight, hemoglobin A1C (HgbA1C; a blood test that indicates whether the level of glucose has been higher than normal in the previous three months), cholesterol, triglycerides, and liver function (all of these can be monitored with a single blood sample) is recommended for anyone on olanzapine, even though our recent study did not identify problematic changes in these measures associated with medication use.

Focusing on: A new medication option

Anorexia nervosa is a complex, dangerous illness. While many patients, especially younger ones with shorter duration of illness, respond to behaviorally focused therapies, others need additional interventions. A recent large study conducted by the authors of this book and their collaborators compared olanzapine to placebo in older adolescent and adult outpatients with anorexia nervosa and found that olanzapine helped participants gain weight at a faster rate than did placebo. Olanzapine is the first medication that has firm evidence to support its use in aiding weight restoration in patients with anorexia nervosa and should be considered when other interventions are insufficient or unavailable.

17

COGNITIVE NEUROSCIENCE

EMERGING KNOWLEDGE ABOUT HOW THE BRAIN WORKS AS APPLIED TO EATING DISORDERS

Cognitive neuroscience is the name of a field of study with the aim of understanding the biological processes that underlie thinking and behavior, with a specific focus on the connections in the brain involved in mental processes. The tools of cognitive neuroscience include neuropsychological assessments, such as standardized measures of attention, memory, or flexibility in thinking, and imaging techniques, such as fMRI (functional magnetic resonance imaging, which measures brain activity by detecting changes associated with blood flow).

This is an exciting avenue of scientific study because it offers us the potential of identifying the mechanisms underlying eating disordered behavior and then developing interventions to target those mechanisms. However, this line of research is relatively new, and it involves complicated techniques, like measuring how people respond to cognitive challenges or tasks while they lie in an MRI machine and obtaining simultaneous pictures of their brain activity. Therefore, we exercise caution in describing what is known relative to what requires further study. Although here we will organize scientific results by thinking processes, no neuropsychological function is truly independent. For example, performance on a decision-making task depends on the individual's ability to attend to the task and to remember instructions.

What types of brain activity are being studied in eating disorders?

Researchers trying to learn more about brain activity among individuals with eating disorders generally focus on the ways in which the brain solves problems. Because eating disorders can be so persistent, there is a lot of interest in a particular process called *executive functioning* (sometimes also called *cognitive control*). Executive functioning is made up of a number of mental processes that allow people to take in new information, process that information, and use it to guide actions according to their goals. Executive functioning is classified into multiple domains (defined in Table 17.1):

- Inhibitory control
- Cognitive flexibility (or set-shifting)
- Central coherence
- Attention bias
- Working memory
- Decision-making

Using this way of thinking about brain activity, we can imagine (and have experienced through our patients) examples of how particular thinking styles manifest in people with eating disorders. For instance, as explained in Chapter 1, a woman with bulimia nervosa may excessively focus on her body weight in evaluating herself as a person, rather than using a range of broader attributes (weak central coherence). A man with anorexia nervosa may attend to an article on the latest fad diet more than to his family's concern about his dangerously low weight (attention bias) and continue to avoid eating fats even though he has reached his initial (low) weight goal and is experiencing physical consequences of this (poor set-shifting).

Table 17.1. Definitions of some areas of executive functioning

Process	Definition
Inhibitory control	• Ability to suppress or interrupt responses • *Cognitive* inhibition is the ability to filter out irrelevant information from working memory. • *Behavioral* inhibition is the ability to withhold an inappropriate motor response (e.g., not to press a button in response to a particular stimulus). • *Reactive* inhibition is the ability to stop an already initiated behavioral response.
Cognitive flexibility (or, set-shifting)	• Ability to shift thoughts or behaviors according to the demands of the situation (e.g., a change in the rules of an ongoing task) • Cognitive flexibility is essential to the regulation of one's behavior in a changing environment. • Poor flexibility is characterized by difficulties with problem-solving and rigid, stereotyped behaviors.
Central coherence	• Degree of focus on details in information processing versus the global integration of information • Weak central coherence is characterized by excessive focus on details (i.e., the trees) relative to broader concepts (i.e., the forest).
Attention bias	• Tendency to over-focus on certain sources of information in the environment
Working memory	• Ability to retain and work with information in mind, using retained information to guide behavior • Comprised of verbal and nonverbal (visual-spatial) components
Decision-making	• Multiple processes including evaluation of a stimulus (i.e., appraisal), selection of a behavior, execution of the behavior, evaluation of the outcome, and formation of a preference

An individual with an eating disorder characterized by binge eating (such as bulimia nervosa or binge-eating disorder) describes being "totally unable to stop eating once I've started" (poor inhibitory control).

While we do not yet know whether and how such processing problems contribute to the beginnings or persistence of eating disorders, we do find some compelling descriptions of patterns in thinking and brain activity reported in scientific studies to date.

Inhibitory control

Research suggests that eating disorders lie on a continuum of inhibition to disinhibition, with restrictive eating disorders such as anorexia nervosa and ARFID characterized by an overly strong inhibition of eating, whereas disorders in which binge eating is prominent (e.g., bulimia nervosa, binge-eating disorder, and their OSFED subthreshold variants—see Chapter 1) are characterized by frequent occasions when there is inadequate inhibition of the urge to eat. Among the binge-eating type disorders, it appears hardest to suppress or interrupt responses when the task involves cues involving foods or related to body weight or shape. But, to highlight the challenges of understanding eating disorders, consider inhibitory control among individuals with the binge/purge subtype of anorexia nervosa. Most of the time, these individuals severely restrict their food intake, implying very strong inhibitory control, but occasionally, they engage in out-of-control binge eating, suggesting a *deficit* in inhibitory control. It is not clear how to understand what appear to be dramatic swings in brain functioning.

Cognitive flexibility (or set-shifting)

Relative to people without eating disorders, individuals with anorexia nervosa, bulimia nervosa, and binge-eating disorder appear to have difficulty adapting their thoughts or behaviors to meet shifting demands of a given situation. This kind of rigidity has been suggested by some scientists to be an inherited biological trait that increases a person's chances of developing anorexia nervosa. It is theorized that this trait contributes to fixed, compulsive behaviors and, indeed, this characteristic has been widely studied and repeatedly described in individuals with this disorder. A number of studies have found deficits in set-shifting among individuals with bulimia nervosa and binge-eating disorder, suggesting that this feature may be relatively nonspecific among eating disorders.

Central coherence

The hypothesis that individuals with eating disorders, and especially those with anorexia nervosa, are very detail focused and have relative difficulty attending to the big picture is supported by several studies.

Attention bias

As described in Chapter 1, several of the eating disorders are diagnosed in part by the presence of an exaggerated focus on body weight, body shape, and food. There is good evidence for this attention bias in women with eating disorders as compared to those without eating disorders. Important cues for individuals with eating disorders include pictures of food, body-related images, and positive and negative words describing body weight and shape. Recent research in this area aims to clarify the nature of the bias (e.g., hyper-awareness of or avoidance of particular cues).

Working memory

Memory in eating disorders is understudied, and most of the existing research has been done in people with anorexia nervosa. The findings are mixed, and few studies have examined the potential impact of other factors on memory, such as starvation, duration of illness, severity of symptoms, or co-occurring psychiatric problems known to influence memory (such as depression and anxiety).

Decision-making

This is an area of robust investigation for eating disorders researchers. This is likely due to core features of these disorders, including:

- The persistence of behaviors despite evidence of the need for change (e.g., compulsive exercise despite injury, or restrictive eating despite seriously low weight)
- The mismatch between goals and behaviors (e.g., binge eating despite a drive for thinness)

There are several themes to the findings in decision-making and eating disorders. First, impulsivity is prominent for individuals with bulimia nervosa. Second, those with anorexia nervosa show a greater ability to delay reward (i.e., delayed discounting performance), and there is some evidence that those with binge-eating disorder show a reduced ability to delay reward, though differences were less common when the comparison group was overweight or obese.

How can cognitive neuroscience inform eating disorder treatment?

The path from the MRI scanner to the treatment room can be long, but exciting. To illustrate, we will describe in some detail a project concerning anorexia nervosa we have been pursuing at Columbia University in the last several years.

The problem

Although the origins of anorexia nervosa are complex and vary from person to person (as described in Chapters 2 and 4), the critical behavioral problem is the same: People with anorexia nervosa do not eat enough to maintain a healthy weight. And many of these individuals, even after they decide they want to get better and eat more, find it very difficult to change their behavior. The question posed from a neuroscience perspective is, "What's going on in the brain?"

The experiment

At first glance, it would seem almost impossible to answer this question, because how can you study what people are NOT doing? However, with the assistance of some leading, very clever neuroscientists, we found a way to reframe the problem by focusing on the decisions people make about what foods to eat. After some twists and turns, we came up with an experiment that shows people 76 pictures of foods. Half of the foods have a higher fat content, like chocolate cake, and half of the foods have a lower fat content, like celery.

Picture this: A person is shown the images on a computer screen three times. The first time, they are shown each picture and asked to rate how healthy they think the food is. The second time, the order of the pictures is scrambled, and the person is again shown each picture and asked to rate how tasty they think the food is. Then, in the third phase, a food that the person rated as neutral both on health and taste is chosen by the experimenter as the reference food. All the foods are shown again, but in pairs, with the reference food always on the left and another food on the right. The person is asked to choose whether they would prefer to eat the food on the right or the food on the left (see Figure 17.1).

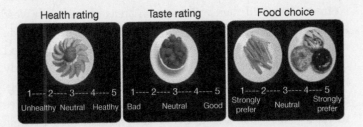

Figure 17.1. Examples of the pictures shown in the three phases of the Food Choice Task.

The results

It turns out, as we had hoped, this relatively simple task gives us a lot of information about people's eating. In a study comparing patterns in those with and without anorexia nervosa, we found that both groups rated high-fat foods as less healthy than low-fat foods. People without anorexia nervosa thought the high-fat foods looked about equally tasty to the low-fat foods, but those with anorexia nervosa thought the high-fat foods were *much* less tasty. And, not surprisingly, individuals with anorexia nervosa were much less likely to choose high-fat foods over the reference food than were the individuals without an eating disorder. Let's say the reference food for a participant with anorexia nervosa was grapes and the reference item for a participant without an eating disorder was yogurt; on average, the person with anorexia nervosa would be much less likely to choose a higher-fat item over grapes than the healthy person would be to choose a higher-fat item than yogurt.

None of this is surprising. In fact, an excellent feature of this task—which involves simply rating pictures of foods—is how well it captures the key behavior of anorexia nervosa, the restriction of the intake of calories.

The brain

To see what's going on in the brain when people make decisions about what to eat, we asked individuals with and without anorexia nervosa to perform this task while they were in an MRI scanner. We could then watch which areas of the brain were active. An important result was that people with anorexia nervosa used different areas of the brain when making food choices. And these areas are ones that appear to be particularly involved in making decisions automatically. These results suggest that, among individuals with anorexia nervosa, the choice to eat low-fat foods and to avoid high-fat foods has become habitual and occurs without a lot of thought.

What this might mean

We doubt that, before the disorder begins, people who go on to develop anorexia nervosa use different areas of their brain to make decisions about what to eat. Rather, we think this change occurs as the illness develops and becomes persistent. This is important, because it suggests that the brain, in some important ways, gets rewired by anorexia nervosa. This does not mean such changes are permanent, but it does suggest how deeply the food restriction is rooted and why it can be so difficult for people to relearn how to eat normally and fully recover.

How we can use our findings to develop new interventions

With results from our experiment in mind, we next asked: If anorexia nervosa is even partially explained by rewiring in the brain, and if this even partially explains the difficulty individuals with the disorder experience in normalizing their eating, could strategies known to help with changing highly automatic behaviors be part of the solution?

To test this idea, we applied a brief behavioral intervention— Regulating Emotions and Changing Habits (REaCH)—to the treatment of anorexia nervosa. In REaCH, study therapists worked with patients to strengthen awareness of the cues preceding their actions, suppress unhelpful habits, create new routines, and practice techniques to cope with the hard parts about behavior change. We compared REaCH to supportive psychotherapy. Twenty-two adults with anorexia nervosa receiving treatment on our inpatient unit participated in the study. The specific intervention they got was chosen at random, but everyone received 12 sessions of their assigned intervention over four weeks of their hospitalization. To see if and how the treatments worked, participants completed questionnaires about habit strength and eating-disordered thoughts and attitudes, and they ate a meal in our research setting at the start and end of the study. We found that the REaCH group experienced greater improvement in habit strength (i.e., lower habit strength) and in eating-disordered thoughts and attitudes than the supportive psychotherapy group. The REaCH group also ate a bit better in our research setting, though this effect was not statistically significant.

This was a proof-of-concept study and the results were encouraging, albeit preliminary. Moving forward, we hope to more vigorously test the intervention. In the meantime, this is an illustrative example of how a line of research that includes cognitive neuroscience can evolve.

Are there other examples?

We are by no means the only group conducting these kinds of studies. In fact, a number of other research groups are pursuing broadly similar lines of research to try to understand what's going on in the brain that supports the development and persistence of eating disorders. Briefly, here are a few examples:

- Investigators at the Mount Sinai School of Medicine in New York City are probing the brain circuits involved in food avoidance and whether individuals with anorexia nervosa may have, from a behavioral perspective, unconsciously learned to view food as disgusting, a perspective that is difficult to unlearn. They are simultaneously testing an intervention that would use principles of interoceptive exposure—in-session practice of physical sensations associated with experiencing disgust—to see if it helps reduce food avoidance.
- Research at the University of Colorado has identified abnormal brain activity in individuals with anorexia nervosa during tasks involving learning, perhaps because of the impact of starvation. These kinds of problems may trigger anxiety and make it harder to change old patterns of thinking and behaving.
- Work at the University of California at San Diego suggests that, even after recovery, women with past histories

of bulimia nervosa show increased positive responses in their brains to small tastes of food compared with women who never had an eating disorder. Perhaps a tendency to react more strongly to sweet tastes makes it more difficult for such individuals to stop eating.

Focusing on: Cognitive neuroscience

In the last several decades, researchers have become more and more sophisticated in their ability to understand how the brain works to make decisions about what behavior to engage in. It is now possible to construct accurate mathematical models about how information is accumulated in (relatively simple) experiments through learning which behaviors yield the most rewards. In recent years, these methods have been extended to behavioral disorders, including eating disorders. This approach, combined with the ability to monitor brain activity using fMRI while humans are actively making decisions about what to do, including about what to eat, offers hope of new and deeper understanding of these disorders and of showing the way for improved treatment.

18

GENETICS

EMERGING KNOWLEDGE ABOUT GENETICS

As we described in Chapter 4, eating disorders tend to run in families. One of the reasons for this is that the genes we inherit from our parents contribute to the risk of developing an eating disorder. Exactly how this works is a hot research topic, not only in the eating disorders field but in all of medicine. In this section, we explore how this research is conducted and what it has revealed so far.

What are genes?

To start with the basics, genes are pieces of DNA and are linked together in thread-like structures called *chromosomes* in the nucleus of every cell. In humans, each cell has 23 pairs of chromosomes; one strand of each pair comes from Mom and the other from Dad. One pair of the 23 chromosomes are the sex chromosomes and differ between men and women: in men, one chromosome in the pair is an X chromosome and one is a Y chromosome; women have two X chromosomes. The DNA in a chromosome is a (very) long string made from four very similar chemical building blocks (molecules) that constitute a four-letter alphabet: A, T, C, and G. Human DNA contains about three billion of these letters and therefore contains an enormous amount of information that, rather miraculously, provides the foundation for each person's uniqueness.

What do our genes do?

The sequence of the A, T, C, and G letters in the DNA spell out instructions that tell the cell how to build specific proteins. There are about 20,000 genes in human DNA that control the production of proteins, but these genes make up only 1–2% of the DNA. The other 99% of the DNA is involved in regulating when, how, and how much protein is made, and some of the DNA is likely silent.

Genes contribute to virtually every aspect of who a person is: how tall they are, their hair color, and what illnesses they are prone to develop.

How are genes studied?

A great deal of scientific effort (and money) has been devoted to the development of methods that allow the contents of someone's DNA to be read quickly and inexpensively. A commonly used method to accomplish this is to detect what are called *single nucleotide polymorphisms*, or SNPs (pronounced "snip"). A SNP occurs when one of the letters in the DNA alphabet differs from what is usually at a single location on a chromosome; for instance, a G may occur where there is usually an A.

SNPs are extremely common, so each person's DNA contains 5–10 million SNPs! Most of these SNPs occur in parts of the DNA that do not lead to the production of proteins and may, therefore, have no functional significance. So, for the most part, they are just innocent markers along the strings of DNA. But, by identifying millions of SNPs, gene mapping techniques can determine to what degree one person's DNA resembles someone else's. This is important, because by using SNPs, we can compare the DNA of people with an illness to the DNA of people without that illness and thereby start to nail down what segments of the DNA contain genes that increase the chances of getting sick.

How do SNPs help scientists figure out where problematic genes are?

Here is a fictional example. Let's imagine someone inherits a problematic gene on chromosome 13 from Mom. And, it turns out that there's a SNP—let's call it SNP#1—on Mom's chromosome 13 that's not far from the problematic gene. If the problem with this gene, all by itself, leads to a disease, and if we sequence the DNA from a lot of people with the disease, we'll find that they tend to have SNP#1 more often than people who don't have the disease—not because SNP#1 is causing the problem, but because it is near the problematic gene. There are a few diseases (e.g., the neurological disorder Huntington's disease) that are caused by a single problem gene, but this pattern of inheritance—called autosomal dominant—is quite rare. In the last few decades, it has become clear that most complex human diseases, like obesity, high blood pressure, and eating disorders, are linked to many SNPs and, therefore, many genes.

What is known about genes and mental disorders, including eating disorders?

In research on mental disorders, the greatest effort has probably been devoted to understanding the genetic contributions to schizophrenia, which is more genetically determined than the eating disorders. The most recent research indicates that variations in at least 250 locations in human DNA contribute to the risk of developing schizophrenia. One important implication is that each single location or gene by itself contributes only very slightly to increasing risk; there are no schizophrenia genes.

Since the effects of a single gene are so small, DNA from enormous numbers of individuals with and without the disorder under study must be obtained. In schizophrenia research, samples may range between 50,000 and 100,000 affected individuals, with similar numbers of individuals without schizophrenia! Again, most of the associations found in this type of research are between the risk of a disorder and a SNP—a marker of a location on a chromosome—not with a gene itself. However, in a few instances the risk gene has been identified, and typically these are genes involved in very basic processes regulating the development of the brain in early life.

In the eating disorders field, virtually all recent genetics research has focused on anorexia nervosa, and large enough studies are only now yielding results. It seems likely that the findings will roughly resemble what has been found for other complex disorders, like schizophrenia—that is, there will be no one anorexia nervosa gene. Rather, there will be multiple locations on multiple chromosomes, each of which contributes slightly to the risk of developing the disorder. It is possible that the genes linked to these locations may be associated with subtle personality characteristics or a person's biological tendency to gain or lose weight. It is also possible that genes may affect how strongly people respond to things that happen in the environment, like the stress of changing to a new school, which sometimes are associated with the beginning of an eating disorder.

In the end, genetic studies may help identify who is at greater risk for eating disorders and who might be helped by early intervention, and perhaps they will help determine which individuals are likely to respond particularly well to a specific type of treatment, such as a particular class of medication (see Chapter 11 for more about different types of medication and how they work).

Focusing on: Genetics

The genes we inherit from our parents play a huge role in determining who we are: our height, our eye color, our personality—virtually every human characteristic. Genes also help determine who is at greater risk of developing most illnesses, including eating disorders. But, it is crucial to emphasize that whatever genes someone inherits do not sentence that person to developing an eating disorder. Genes interact with each other and with many things that happen as we live our lives and, in some very complex way, contribute a bit to who is more likely to develop a problem with their eating and who is not.

RESOURCES

Books

Astrachan-Fletcher, Ellen, and Michael Maslar. *The Dialectical Behavior Therapy Skills Workbook for Bulimia: Using DBT to Break the Cycle and Regain Control of Your Life*. Oakland, California: New Harbinger Publications, 2009.

Brown, Harriet. *Brave Girl Eating: A Family's Struggle with Anorexia.* New York: Harper Collins Publishers, 2010.

Crosbie, Casie, and Wendy Sterling. *How to Nourish Your Child Through an Eating Disorder: A Simple, Plate-by-Plate Approach to Rebuilding a Healthy Relationship with Food*. New York: The Experiment Publishing, 2018.

Fairburn, Christopher G. *Overcoming Binge Eating: The Proven Program to Learn Why You Binge and How You Can Stop*. 2nd edition. New York: Guilford Press, 2013.

Liu, Aimee. *Gaining: The Truth about Life after Eating Disorders*. New York: Hachette Book Group, 2008.

Liu, Aimee. *Restoring Our Bodies, Reclaiming Our Lives: Guidance and Reflections on Recovery from Eating Disorders*. Boston, Massachusetts: Trumpeter Books, 2011.

Lock, James, and Daniel Le Grange. *Help Your Teenager Beat an Eating Disorder*. 2nd edition. New York: Guilford Press, 2015.

Muhlheim, Lauren. *When Your Teen Has an Eating Disorder: Practical Strategies to Help Your Teen Recover from Anorexia, Bulimia, and Binge Eating*. Oakland, California: New Harbinger, 2018.

Safer, Debra L., Sarah Adler, and Philip C. Masson. *The DBT Solution for Emotional Eating: A Proven Program to Break the Cycle of Bingeing and Out-of-Control Eating.* New York: Guilford Press, 2018.

Schaefer, Jenni. *Goodbye ED, Hello Me: Recover from Your Eating Disorder and Fall in Love with Life.* New York: McGraw Hill, 2009.

Schaefer, Jenni. *Life without ED: How One Woman Declared Independence from Her Eating Disorder and How You Can Too.* New York: McGraw Hill, 2004.

Taitz, Jennifer L. *End Emotional Eating: Using Dialectical Behavior Therapy Skills to Cope with Difficult Emotions and Develop a Healthy Relationship to Food.* Oakland, California: New Harbinger Publications, 2012.

Thomas, Jennifer J., and Jenni Schaefer. *Almost Anorexic: Is My (or My Loved One's) Relationship with Food a Problem?* Center City, Minnesota: Hazelden/Harvard University, 2013.

Waller, Glenn, Victoria Mountford, Rachel Lawson, Emma Gray, Helen Cordery, and Hendrik Hinrichsen. *Beating Your Eating Disorder: A Cognitive-Behavioral Self-Help Guide for Adult Sufferers and Their Carers.* Cambridge, United Kingdom: Cambridge University Press, 2010.

Walsh, B. Timothy, and Deborah R. Glasofer. *If Your Adolescent Has an Eating Disorder: An Essential Resource for Parents (Adolescent Mental Health Initiative).* 2nd edition. New York: Oxford University Press, May 2020.

Wilhelm, Sabine. *Feeling Good about the Way You Look: A Program for Overcoming Body Image Problems.* New York: Guilford Press, 2006.

Other Materials

Anorexia, Parents-to-Parents: What We Wish We Had Understood. Documentary available online at http://www.parents-to-parents. org/

Around the Dinner Table. Online support forum for parents and carers of those with eating disorders, offered and moderated by Families Empowered and Supporting Treatment for Eating Disorders (F.E.A.S.T.), available at https://www.aroundthedinnertable.org/

Breathe2Relax. T2 (The National Center of Telehealth and Technology) [mobile application software].

Calm. Calm.com, Inc. [mobile application software].

CBT Thought Record Diary. MoodTools [mobile application software].

DBT Diary Card + Skills Coach. Durham DBT, Inc. [mobile application software].

MoodTools. MoodTools [mobile application software].

MindShift. Anxiety Canada Association [mobile application software].

Parent, Educator and Coach Toolkits. Free educational resources by the National Eating Disorders Association, available online for download at https://www.nationaleatingdisorders.org/toolkits-0

Recovery Record. Recovery Record [mobile application software].

Rise Up + Recover. Recovery Warriors, LLC. [mobile application software].

Hot Research Topics: Academic Articles

Chapter 16: Olanzapine: A New Medication for Anorexia Nervosa

Attia, E., J. Steinglass, B. T. Walsh, Y. Wang, P. Wu, C. Schreyer, J. Wildes, Z. Yilmaz, A. Guarda, A. Kaplan, and M. Marcus. Olanzapine versus Placebo in Outpatient Adults with Anorexia Nervosa: A Randomized Clinical Trial. *American Journal of Psychiatry.* 2019; 176:449–456.

Chapter 17: Cognitive Neuroscience: Emerging Knowledge about How the Brain Works as Applied to Eating Disorders

Foerde, K., J. Steinglass, D. Shohamy, and B. T. Walsh. Neural Mechanisms Supporting Maladaptive Food Choices in Anorexia Nervosa. *Nature Neuroscience.* 2015; 18:1571–1573.

Steinglass, J. E., L. A. Berner, and E. Attia. Cognitive Neuroscience of Eating Disorders. *Psychiatric Clinics of North America.* 2019; 42:75–91.

Chapter 18: Genetics: Emerging Knowledge about Genetics

Bulik, C. M., L. Blake, and J. Austin. Genetics of Eating Disorders: What the Clinician Needs to Know. *Psychiatric Clinics of North America.* 2019; 42(1):59–73.

Organizations

Academy for Eating Disorders (AED)
(703) 234-4079
Email: info@aedweb.org
https://www.aedweb.org

Beat Eating Disorders
0300 123-3355
Email: help@beateatingdisorders.org.uk
http://www.beateatingdisorders.org.uk

Eating Disorders Coalition (EDC)
(202) 543-9570
http://www.eatingdisorderscoalition.org

Eating Disorders Referral and Information Center
https://www.edreferral.com

Families Empowered and Supporting Treatment for Eating Disorders
(F.E.A.S.T.)
U.S. (855) 50-FEAST
Canada +1 647-247-1339
Australia +61 731886675
U.K. +44 3308280031
New Zealand +64 98875172
Israel +972 23748988
Email: info@feast-ed.org
https://www.feast-ed.org/

Maudsley Parents
http://www.maudsleyparents.org/

NAMI: National Alliance on Mental Illness
(703) 524-7600
Email: info@nami.org
https://www.nami.org

National Eating Disorders Association (NEDA)
(800) 931-2237
Email: info@NationalEatingDisorders.org
https://www.nationaleatingdisorders.org

National Eating Disorder Information Centre—Canada (NEDIC)
(866) 633-4230 (toll-free in Canada) or (416) 340-4156 (Toronto)
https://nedic.ca

Obesity Society
(301) 563-6526
https://www.obesity.org

Project HEAL
Email: contact@theprojectheal.org
https://www.theprojectheal.org/

INDEX

Tables, figures and boxes are indicated by *t*, *f* and *b* following the page number

For the benefit of digital users, indexed terms that span two pages (e.g., 52–53) may, on occasion, appear on only one of those pages.